THIS IS HISTORY.

The Impact of Empire

**A WORLD STUDY OF THE BRITISH EMPIRE –
1585 TO THE PRESENT**

THE SCHOOLS HISTORY PROJECT

S·H·P

OFFICIAL TEXT

THIS IS HISTORY!

The Impact of Empire

A WORLD STUDY OF THE BRITISH EMPIRE –
1585 TO THE PRESENT

**MICHAEL
RILEY**

**JAMIE
BYROM**

**CHRISTOPHER
CULPIN**

JOHN MURRAY

The Schools History Project

The Project was set up in 1972, with the aim of improving the study of History for students aged 13–16. This involved a reconsideration of the ways in which History contributes to the educational needs of young people. The Project devised new objectives, new criteria for planning and developing courses, and the materials to support them. New examinations, requiring new methods of assessment, also had to be developed. These have continued to be popular. The advent of GCSE in 1987 led to the expansion of Project approaches into other syllabuses.

The Schools History Project has been based at Trinity and All Saints College, Leeds, since 1978, from where it supports teachers through a biennial Bulletin, regular INSET, an annual Conference and a website (www.tasc.ac.uk/shp).

Since the National Curriculum was drawn up in 1991, the Project has continued to expand its publications, bringing its ideas to courses for Key Stage 3 as well as a range of GCSE and A level specifications.

Note: The wording and sentence structure of some written sources have been adapted and simplified to make them accessible to all pupils, while faithfully preserving the sense of the original.

Words printed in SMALL CAPITALS are defined in the glossary on page 119.

The Indian cities of Bombay, Madras and Calcutta are now known as Mumbai, Chennai and Kolkata respectively. Throughout this book we have chosen to use the old names as these were used in the period being studied.

© Michael Riley, Jamie Byrom, Christopher Culpin 2004
First published in 2004 by
John Murray (Publishers) Ltd, a member of the Hodder Headline Group
338 Euston Road
London NW1 3BH

Reprinted 2004

Layouts by Liz Rowe
Artwork by Art Construction, Peter Bull, Jon Davis (Linden Artists), Richard Duszczak, Tony Randell, Steve Smith, Craig Warwick (Linden Artists)
Typeset in Goudy by Fakenham Photosetting
Printed and bound in Spain by Bookprint, S.L., Barcelona

A catalogue entry for this book is available from the British Library

Pupil's Book ISBN 0 7195 8561 9
Teacher's Resource Book ISBN 0 7195 8562 7

◆ Contents

SOURCE 1 A map of the world published in 1886.

This map was made in Britain in 1886. The land shaded in pink made up the British Empire at that time. Britannia – the symbol of Britain – is shown sitting on top of the world. Other figures represent the different people who lived and worked within the British Empire.

ACTIVITY

Study Source 1 carefully. Note that a small map of the Empire in 1786 is included. Look at the different types of people shown around the border and at the lines drawn across the seas. Now answer this question:

'What messages is the map trying to give about the British Empire?'

This book tells the story of the British Empire. It is not just a story about land; it's a story about people. The Empire's growth and decline deeply affected people's lives. In the enquiries in this book you will find out who made the Empire, who suffered from it, who enjoyed it, who hated it, and who benefited from it. That's why the book is called *The Impact of Empire*. Many of the issues you will find out about are still the subject of argument, sometimes bitter argument. We hope that this book will help to get you involved in some of these issues and to make up your own mind about them.

But before you go any further, you need to see the 'Big Picture'. Here is a very short and simple summary of the story of the British Empire. Read it carefully and then tackle the activity on page 5. This should help you make more sense of the detailed enquiries that follow in the rest of the book.

SOURCE 2 An English painting of a Native American, 1585.

The Empire's story

Stage 1: First contacts

In 1450 different CIVILIZATIONS flourished across the world. These civilizations had little contact with each other, but all this was soon to change. At the end of the fifteenth century Europeans began to explore the rest of the world.

The Portuguese and Spanish led the way. Then, in 1585, sailors and adventurers set up England's first COLONY at Roanoke in North America. Other colonies followed.

From their very first meeting, Native Americans (Source 2) and English COLONISTS changed each others' lives. The English brought to America new ideas about farming, new weapons, a new religion, a new language ... and new diseases that killed large numbers of Native Americans. When they returned home, English men and women took paintings and stories of the wonders of this 'New World' as well as new foods and new plants.

Stage 2: People on the move

During the seventeenth and eighteenth centuries growing numbers of people began to move from all over Europe to set up colonies in different parts of the world. Many British people settled along the east coast of North America. Some people owned PLANTATIONS in America or in the West Indies. European traders took millions of Africans across the Atlantic Ocean to be sold as slaves who would work on the plantations. Many white people began to treat black people as second class human beings.

Britain's trade with America and the West Indies made her rich. So did her trade in India. British traders took control of large parts of India when rival traders from France or local Indian princes tried to force them out. In Australia, many of the first British colonists were convicts who had been sent there as a punishment.

SOURCE 3 A painting of a British ship carrying convicts to Australia in the 1800s.

Stage 3: World Empire

During the nineteenth century European powers fought to gain control of different parts of the world. Africa was divided up between them in the last few years of the century. The Europeans drew up borders and created new nations which ignored ancient tribal areas. British farmers and miners moved into some of the richest land in Africa.

By 1900 the British Empire covered a fifth of the world and Britain ruled a quarter of the world's population. The British proudly claimed that, wherever they ruled, they imposed English laws and English customs, preaching Christianity and running schools and hospitals for the native peoples.

SOURCE 4 An African war scene, 1879.

Stage 4: The Empire ends

During the second half of the twentieth century European countries gave up their colonies. Quite often it took violent rebellions by native people to make the Europeans give up power. Gradually, more and more countries gained INDEPENDENCE from their colonial rulers. In 1948 the British left India. Then, during the 1950s and 1960s, the British Empire collapsed completely. Native people such as the African leader in Source 5 regained control of their own lands. Despite this, Britain's influence can still be seen in the language, laws and forms of government that are used in the many parts of the world that used to be part of the British Empire.

SOURCE 5   An African independence ceremony, 1963.

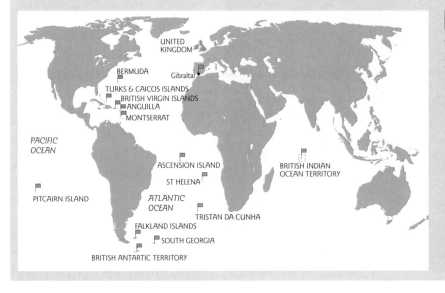

UNITED KINGDOM
BERMUDA
Gibraltar
TURKS & CAICOS ISLANDS
BRITISH VIRGIN ISLANDS
ANGUILLA
MONTSERRAT
PACIFIC OCEAN
ASCENSION ISLAND
ST HELENA
BRITISH INDIAN OCEAN TERRITORY
PITCAIRN ISLAND
ATLANTIC OCEAN
TRISTAN DA CUNHA
FALKLAND ISLANDS
SOUTH GEORGIA
BRITISH ANTARTIC TERRITORY

SOURCE 6 A map of the world today, showing British territory in red.

A CTIVITY

Look back over the four stages of the Empire's story (pages 3–5). Use the information in the story to make a list of all the ways in which the British Empire had an **impact** on the world.

Now you should be familiar with the 'Big Picture' of the British Empire. It's time to turn to the details by tackling the enquiries in the rest of the book.

ROANOKE: WHAT WENT WRONG WITH ENGLAND'S FIRST COLONY?

Decide for yourself why it failed

Our history of the British Empire begins in 1585 with this man – Walter Raleigh. Look closely at the portrait and think of three good words to describe Raleigh.

AETATIS SVÆ 34
AN 1588

AMOR ET VIRTUTE

SOURCE I A portrait of Sir Walter Raleigh, 1588.

Walter Raleigh was very rich and very powerful. At the beginning of 1585 he was also very excited. For some years he had been the favourite of Queen Elizabeth I. The Queen adored Raleigh and she showered him with gifts of money and property. In the spring of 1585 Raleigh made bold plans for spending some of his vast fortune.

He decided that he would send about 300 English people to live in North America. Raleigh wanted to go down in history as the man who established England's first colony. This would be the first English settlement in the unexplored land across the Atlantic Ocean. Nobody in England had attempted anything like this before. Nobody knew whether the plan would succeed.

◆ *Mystery*

In the sixteenth century Europeans knew very little about North America. Spanish merchants had set up trading posts on the islands of the Caribbean (West Indies). They had also conquered the Aztec Empire in central America and destroyed the Inca Empire in Peru. But North America remained much more of a mystery. A few English merchants had sailed across the Atlantic, hoping to make their fortunes by trading with the Native Americans who lived there. They had all returned disappointed.

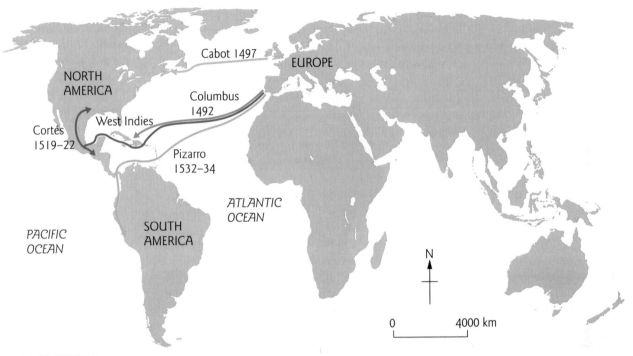

SOURCE 2 European exploration and conquest of the Americas.

Walter Raleigh was fascinated by America. He read everything he could find about the strange people who lived in this 'New World'. He was keen to ensure that his own colonists did not treat the Native Americans as brutally as the Spaniards had done.

In 1584, to discover more about this distant land, and to find a suitable place for England's first colony, Raleigh organised a voyage to America. His men explored the North American coast and found the perfect place – Roanoke.

Roanoke was an island. It was fertile and richly stocked with wildlife. It was sheltered from the Atlantic storms and hidden from Spanish ships by banks of sand dunes. The Native Americans who lived on Roanoke were very friendly towards the strange white people in the big ships. When Raleigh's men returned to England they even brought two Native Americans – Wancheso and Manteo – back to London with them.

YOUR ENQUIRY

In the months that followed, Sir Walter Raleigh made careful preparations to ensure that England's first colony was a success. In fact, the colony was a disaster! In this enquiry you are going to find out why and explain what went wrong.

If you wish: Before you go any further, discuss the things that you think might go wrong. Make a list, then go back to it later to see how right or wrong you were!

◆ The preparations

As Raleigh began to make detailed plans he realised that establishing a colony in America was going to be a huge challenge. It was like taking a whole English village and planting it in an unknown land. Raleigh thought hard about some of the problems he faced.

Raleigh's problems

PROBLEM 1: How will I pay for the colony?

Raleigh's first and greatest problem was how to raise enough money to pay for the ships and supplies. The Queen offered one of her ships, the *Tiger*, and gave Raleigh £400 worth of gunpowder from the Tower of London. But Raleigh needed a lot more than this and he did not want to use up all of his own money.

PROBLEM 2: How can I persuade people to go?

Raleigh needed about 600 people for the voyage. Half of these would stay in America to set up the colony. When Raleigh began recruiting, he found that it was difficult to persuade people to join the voyage. It was particularly hard to find ordinary sailors as many were afraid of being captured and tortured by the Spanish.

PROBLEM 3: Who should lead the colony?

Raleigh needed brave and intelligent people to lead his expedition. An experienced commander should lead the voyage. A trusted governor should be in charge of setting up the colony. A respected scholar and painter should make a detailed record of the strange people, beasts and plants of the 'New World'.

PROBLEM 4: What food and supplies will the colony need to get started?

If the colonists were lucky enough to arrive in spring, they would be able to sow their crops. However, they would still need enough food supplies to last them the five months until the crops could be harvested. The colonists would also need to take materials to build a fort. There was no stone near Roanoke and Raleigh wondered if the colonists should take stone from England.

PROBLEM 5: How should we treat the Native Americans?

Roanoke island was already inhabited by Native Americans. They had been friendly to Raleigh's men when they first visited Roanoke but nobody really knew how they would react to people actually coming to live on their land. Raleigh knew that thousands of Aztecs and Incas had lost their lives in the Spanish conquest of their land in Central and South America. He would need to make sure that the English colonists lived on good terms with these Native Americans.

ACTIVITY A

Which of these problems do you think Raleigh was unable to solve by using his money?

Raleigh's solutions

Raleigh was pleased with the solutions he found. But, if you think carefully, you will probably be able to think of some of the things that might go wrong with Raleigh's plans.

SOLUTION 1: paying for the colony

Raleigh decided that he had to persuade English merchants to lend him money to pay for the new colony. He promised the investors a share of the loot from any Spanish ships that could be raided on the way to America. Wealthy merchants soon began to invest in the project.

SOLUTION 2: persuading people to go

Raleigh asked the Queen for sweeping new powers to force men into service on his ships. Elizabeth gave her permission and sailors in the ports of the West Country were forced into service against their will.

SOLUTION 3: choosing the leaders

Raleigh had little trouble finding a commander for his expedition. **Richard Grenville** had two essential qualities: he loved adventure and he hated Spain. However, he also had a fiery temper and a liking for too much good wine. Apart from a short sail across the English Channel, the voyage to America was Richard Grenville's first attempt at seamanship.

The governor of England's first colony was to be **Ralph Lane**, an expert on building forts and a man who enjoyed a hard life.

Raleigh hired **John White**, a talented artist, to record the expedition.

Finally, **Thomas Harriot**, Raleigh's friend from Oxford University, was employed to study and to map the new territory. Harriot was the only person who could communicate with **Wancheso** and **Manteo**, the Native Americans who were returning to Roanoke with the colonists.

SOLUTION 4: food and supplies

Raleigh thought very carefully about the food and supplies (or PROVISIONS) which the new colony would need. Meat, fish, grain and other foods were packed onto the ships with great care so that they would not rot. Large quantities of beer, cider and wine were loaded. Herbs and medicines were carefully packed.

No one knew much about the soils on Roanoke and so a variety of seeds were taken, to be sure that some would grow.

The quantity of provisions was impressive, but it was nowhere near enough. Grenville would have to stop in the Caribbean to stock up on salt, fruit and livestock. This was not going to be easy as every port was controlled by the Spanish who were under strict orders not to sell anything to the English.

SOLUTION 5: avoiding brutality

Raleigh declared that there were to be severe punishments for anyone who:

– hit a Native American
– forced a Native American to work against his or her will
– entered the house of a Native American without his or her permission
– raped a Native American woman.

ACTIVITY B

What a mess! There were so many reasons why the colony at Roanoke might go wrong.

Hang on a minute! Raleigh got a lot right. There were plenty of reasons why the colony at Roanoke stood a good chance of succeeding.

Use the information on these two pages to find reasons to support each of these views.

◆ The voyage to Roanoke

7 Two weeks after leaving Hispaniola the expedition reached the coast of North America. A storm threatened. Even in good weather shallow sandbanks made this stretch of coastline near Roanoke extremely dangerous. Disaster struck. The ships hit a sandbank just as the storm began. For more than two hours the *Tiger* was battered by huge waves. The sailors' lives were spared, but when they hauled the wreck of the *Tiger* onto the beach, their hearts sank. The seawater had ruined nearly all their supplies. The colonists would now have to rely on the Native Americans for food.

ATLANTIC OCEAN

Roanoke Island

5 When the *Tiger* arrived in Puerto Rico Grenville was bitterly disappointed. Not one of the other English ships had arrived. The tropical heat now ruined what little food was left. The sailors ate biscuits infested with weevil. They drank the water with their teeth clenched to strain out the worms. Many men became sick. To make matters worse they were now in hostile Spanish territory. Fortunately another of the fleet's ships, the *Elizabeth*, soon arrived in Puerto Rico.

NORTH AMERICA

6 On 1 June 1585 the *Tiger* and the *Elizabeth* arrived at the island of Hispaniola. This was the colonists' last hope of obtaining food before they reached the North American mainland. Manteo warned the colonists that food was always scarce on Roanoke in winter. It was essential that they obtained animals and seedlings in the Caribbean. Grenville and his men were surprised to find a warm welcome from the Spanish governor of Hispaniola. The governor supplied the colonists with everything they needed, together with large quantities of sugar, ginger and pearls.

PUERTO RICO

HISPANIOLA

CARIBBEAN SEA

N

4 Twenty-one days after leaving England the *Tiger* arrived in the Caribbean. It was now so hot that several of the sailors dived into the surf. This was a terrible mistake. One poor man had his leg bitten off by a shark. He screamed in pain as the stump was dipped in boiling tar to CAUTERISE it.

SOUTH AMERICA

0   1000   2000   3000 km

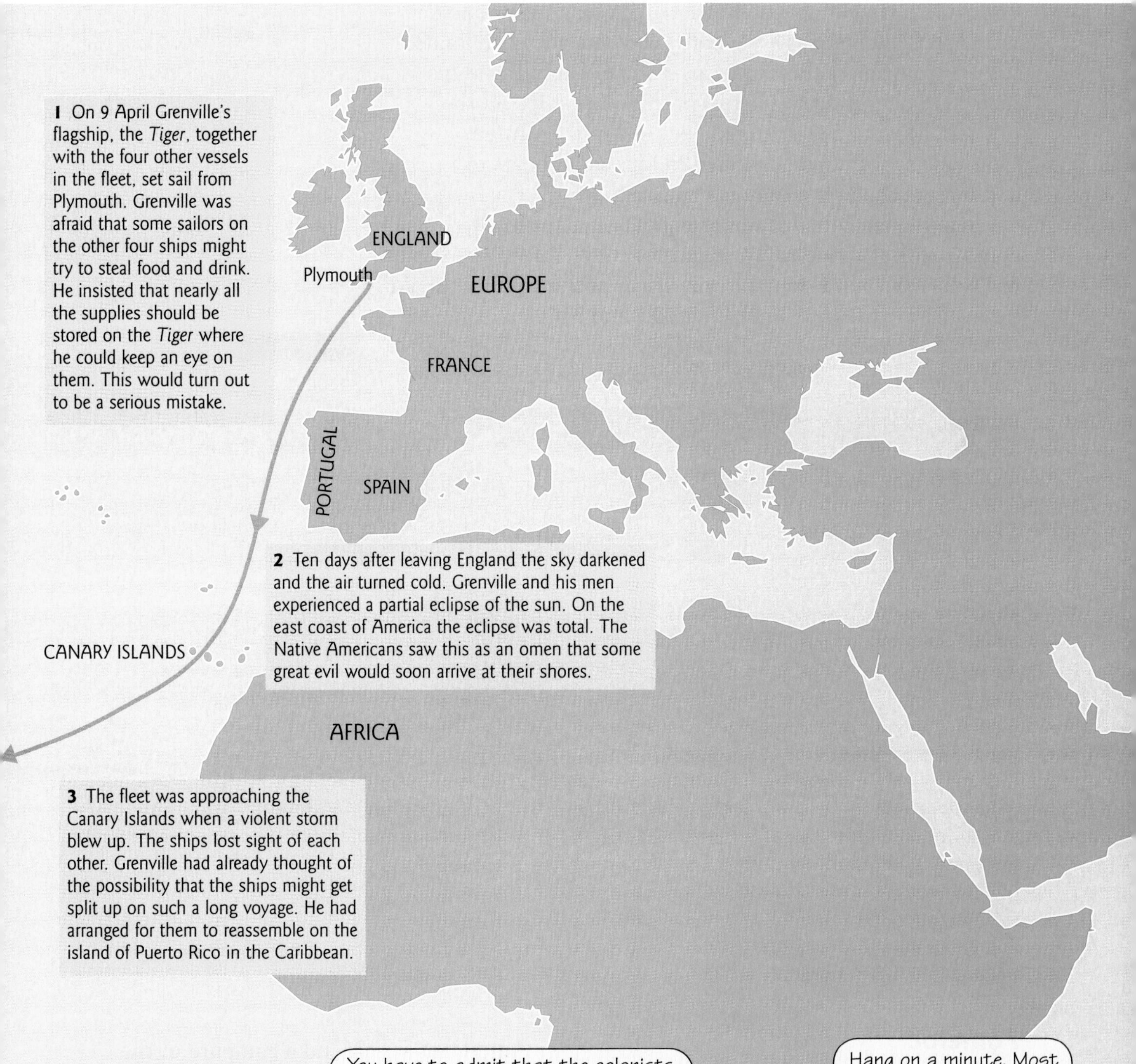

1 On 9 April Grenville's flagship, the *Tiger*, together with the four other vessels in the fleet, set sail from Plymouth. Grenville was afraid that some sailors on the other four ships might try to steal food and drink. He insisted that nearly all the supplies should be stored on the *Tiger* where he could keep an eye on them. This would turn out to be a serious mistake.

ENGLAND

Plymouth

EUROPE

FRANCE

PORTUGAL

SPAIN

2 Ten days after leaving England the sky darkened and the air turned cold. Grenville and his men experienced a partial eclipse of the sun. On the east coast of America the eclipse was total. The Native Americans saw this as an omen that some great evil would soon arrive at their shores.

CANARY ISLANDS

AFRICA

3 The fleet was approaching the Canary Islands when a violent storm blew up. The ships lost sight of each other. Grenville had already thought of the possibility that the ships might get split up on such a long voyage. He had arranged for them to reassemble on the island of Puerto Rico in the Caribbean.

> You have to admit that the colonists had some good luck on the voyage.

> Hang on a minute. Most things that went wrong were just bad luck.

ACTIVITY

Think carefully about the events of the voyage. Find examples to support each of these views.

> Yes, but they made a lot of mistakes on the voyage too.

◆ First encounters

Grenville planned to settle Raleigh's colonists on Roanoke Island, 100 kilometres to the north of where they had landed.

A few days after the disastrous storm Grenville and his men were overjoyed to see two of their lost ships on the horizon. Most of the scattered fleet was now reunited. Grenville set off with sixty men in four small boats to explore the shallow waters of Pamlico Sound.

Grenville knew that it was essential to make friendly contact with the Native Americans who lived along the shores of Pamlico Sound. It was the only way that the colonists could survive. Over the next week Grenville and his men explored over 300 kilometres of coastline. They visited the three Native American villages of Pomeioc, Aquascogoc and Secotan.

SOURCE 3 The area around Roanoke.

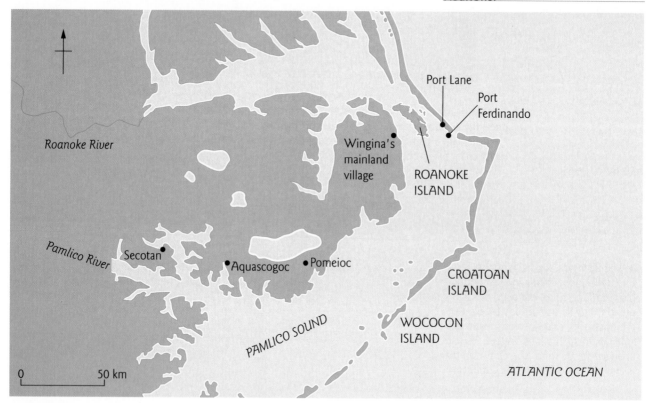

Pomeioc

After a hard day's rowing through the swamps, the colonists landed near the small settlement of Pomeioc. They pulled the boats ashore, picked up their MUSKETS and nervously set off for the village. As the colonists approached Pomeioc they saw longhouses built from rough poles and covered in mats. A group of Native Americans sat around a campfire in the middle of the village.

The colonists were amazed by the appearance of these people. The men wore deerskin around their waists. Their hair was shaven to form a crest on top of their heads. The women also wore deerskin, but did not cover their breasts. They had shaved hair and tattoos on their cheeks.

John White set to work painting this watercolour of a woman and child (Source 4). The child was frightened by John White's beard, but stood still to allow him to paint her when he gave her an English doll.

SOURCE 4 John White's painting of a Native American woman and her child.

Aquascogoc

It was at the next village, Aquascogoc, that something went dreadfully wrong. The Native Americans here did not seem pleased to see the Englishmen, and so the colonists returned quickly to their boats. It was only later that Grenville noticed that his silver drinking cup was missing. He was furious and sent his men back to the village to have his revenge. The Native Americans had fled, but the Englishmen set fire to the village and to the corn which surrounded it. This was a very hasty and foolish thing to do. After all, the colonists would soon have to depend on the native people for food.

Secotan

The last village the colonists visited was Secotan (see Source 5). The Native Americans here were thought to be hostile, so some of the English wore full armour. They were surprised to be welcomed by a friendly chieftain who arranged an evening of entertainment. The colonists enjoyed the feast. They were amazed by the strange dances which the Native American men and women performed around a circle of posts carved with weird human heads.

Secotan was very similar to Pomeioc, apart from a large building with a barrel-shaped roof. When Thomas Harriot asked to be taken inside he found himself surrounded by mummified corpses. This was the 'charnel house' where the Native Americans mummified the bodies of their dead relatives, in order to preserve them for the after-life.

ACTIVITY

Look at Source 5 on page 15.
1 What details of life in Secotan did John White include in his painting?
2 What does the painting suggest about John White's attitude towards Native Americans?
3 In what ways does White seem to have differed from Grenville in his attitude and behaviour towards the Native Americans?

SOURCE 5 John White's painting of Secotan.

Their rype corne

Their greene corne

Corne newly sprong.

Their sitting at meate

The place of solemne prayer

The howse wherin the Tombe of their Herounds standeth.

SECOTON·

A Ceremony in their prayers wth strange iestures and songes dansing abowt posts carued on the topps lyke mens faces.

◆ The English settlement on Roanoke

At the end of July 1585, Grenville and his men returned from their expedition around Pamlico Sound. They sailed north to Port Ferdinando where they began to unload supplies for their planned settlement on Roanoke. Grenville knew that the colonists could only settle on the island if the Native Americans agreed. The chief of the local tribes, Chief Wingina, was recovering from a war wound, so Grenville met with the chief's brother. The two men agreed that the colonists should settle on the north-eastern part of Roanoke, near Shallowbag Bay.

Ralph Lane now took up his role as the colony's governor. When all the supplies were unloaded, Lane started the urgent task of building a fort. There was no stone on Roanoke, so Lane was forced to build a fort from a deep ditch, banks of sand and timbers. When the fort was finished, Lane ordered the men to start work on the other buildings. Ralph Lane and the other gentlemen had decent houses, but the rest of the men lived in rough wooden shacks. They then worked on the church, storehouse, armoury, stables and jail. By the third week in August the building work was complete. Grenville set sail for England as planned, leaving 107 colonists behind. This was a smaller number than Raleigh had planned, but more realistic given the shortage of supplies.

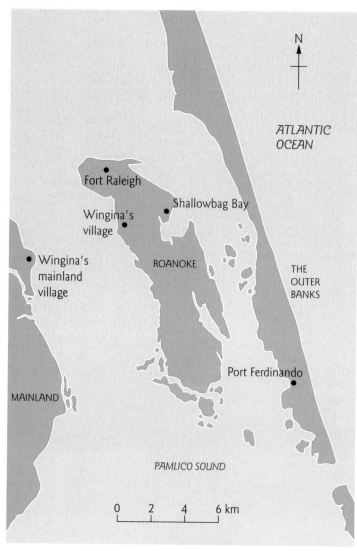

SOURCE 6 A map of Roanoke.

The colonists' links with England were now broken. They were totally alone. Their food supplies were very low and they began to fear the future. The colonists began to disagree among themselves. Many did not share Ralph Lane's enjoyment of hardship: there were too many gentlemen who were not used to hard work. Over half the colonists were soldiers and some of these men began to behave badly. Lane punished them harshly. At least one soldier was hanged. His rotting corpse was left hanging from a tree as a warning to others.

A few weeks later, the colonists received their first visit from Chief Wingina. They were keen to meet this powerful chief, who ruled over all the Native Americans on Roanoke as well as a small settlement on the mainland.

Wingina was wary of the English colonists. He knew that many Native Americans had died shortly after a visit from the Englishmen. Wingina thought that this might be because the colonists had supernatural powers. In fact, some of the colonists were carrying measles and smallpox, and the Native Americans had no immunity to these European diseases. Wingina also knew that the English colonists would be forced to depend on his people for food during the coming winter months: the colonists had arrived at Roanoke too late to plant any seeds; they found it difficult to shoot animals in the forest because so much of their gunpowder was damp; and they were useless at catching fish in the shallow waters of Pamlico Sound.

Through the winter of 1585–86 the bellies of the English settlers ached with hunger. Wingina and his people helped the colonists to set traps to catch fish; they also supplied them with corn, but the Native Americans too were running short of food. Wingina began to lose patience with the colonists.

SOURCE 7   One of John White's paintings. The man is believed to be Chief Wingina.

The manner of their attire and painting them selues when they goe to their generall huntings or at theire Solemne feasts.

ACTIVITY

1 What does the painting (Source 7) suggest about John White's attitude towards Chief Wingina?
2 Think carefully about what went wrong when the colonists settled on Roanoke. Find examples to support each of these views:

> I think Ralph Lane was the main reason why the colony failed.

> Hang on! There were lots of other reasons why things went wrong.

17

◆ A bloody end

The chief decided that there was only one solution – to wipe out the English settlement. Wingina moved his base to the mainland. He then ordered his men to destroy the fish traps they had set for the colonists. With the colonists now weakened, the chief planned his attack on the English fort.

Ralph Lane heard about Wingina's planned attack from a Native American who was friendly to the English colonists. Lane decided to attack first. Just after dawn on 1 June 1586 he led 27 of his men across the water towards Wingina's mainland settlement. He pretended that he simply wanted to talk with Wingina. When Lane and the English soldiers entered the village they saw Wingina and several village elders sitting around the campfire. The soldiers fired their muskets straight into the group of men.

SOURCE 8 A woodcut showing the attack on Wingina's village.

Wingina was the first to be hit. The colonists thought he was dead, but the chief suddenly sprang to his feet and ran into the forest. A band of soldiers set off after him. One of the soldiers caught sight of Wingina and fired his pistol. He hit the chief on the buttocks, but Wingina was not badly injured and he ran on. He had now shaken off all but two of the soldiers, and they were finding it difficult to run through the forest in their heavy clothes.

Ralph Lane waited anxiously in the village. He had no idea whether Wingina was alive or dead. After a long time, the two exhausted soldiers emerged from the forest. Lane saw that one of them was clutching something in his hand – the bloody head of Chief Wingina.

The death of Wingina meant that the English colony was now safe from Native American attack. But good relations between the English settlers and the Native Americans were in ruins. In the end this did not matter to the colonists on Roanoke. Within a few days the settlers would be on their way back home. England's first colony would be abandoned.

The colony abandoned

On 10 June the colonists awoke to a wonderful sight. Twenty-three English ships were anchored off the coast. Sir Francis Drake had brought a fleet of ships to rescue Raleigh's starving colony on Roanoke.

The departure of the colonists from Roanoke was chaotic. Nearly all the charts, notes, maps, specimens, paintings and seeds were dropped in the sea. But these records of the 'New World' were not the only things to be left behind. In the rush to leave before a storm began, Drake's fleet set off for England leaving three of the colonists on the island. What became of these men is a mystery which has never been solved.

So, in 1586, England's first colony ended in failure. In the years that followed other groups of colonists would attempt to settle in America. Eventually they would succeed. During the seventeenth century a string of European colonies would grow up along the east coast of America. And many more Native Americans would die from the white men's diseases and guns.

ACTIVITY

Roanoke failed mainly because the colonists were so poorly prepared. It was doomed from the start.

I disagree. In so many ways the colonists were simply unlucky.

I think you are both missing the point. The main reason Roanoke went wrong was because of the attitude and behaviour of some of the colonists towards the Native Americans.

Think carefully about the end of the colony. Find examples to support each of these views.

FINAL ACTIVITY

The editor of a history magazine has asked you to write an article for the next issue. The title will be, 'What went wrong with England's first colony?' Use the notes that you have made in the activities for this chapter to write the article. You can make your article really good by:

◆ telling the story of Roanoke in an interesting way
◆ giving your own clear explanation of what went wrong
◆ selecting three interesting pictures for your article.

2 'ACCIDENTAL RULERS?': HOW DID THE BRITISH TAKE CONTROL OF INDIA?

Play the East India Company Trading Game to find out

In 1600, fourteen years after the failure of the Roanoke colony, a group of Tudor merchants started an organisation that was to change the history of the world. They called it the East India Company (EIC). At the time, these men had no idea just how powerful their new company was to become. All they wanted to do was trade with India to make themselves rich.

But, in history, what people intend and what actually happens are often two very different things.

In 1608 the East India Company sent its first ship on the long voyage to India. The London merchants waited eagerly for its return. They hoped that it would be full of fine silks, spices and jewels. They also hoped that its captain, Sir William Hawkins, would have won the friendship of the great Indian ruler, the Mughal emperor. They were to be sadly disappointed.

When the ship finally returned in 1612 the crew reported that ...

- ◆ they had collected very few valuable goods
- ◆ rival traders from Portugal had tried to murder Hawkins in India
- ◆ Indian officials had taken away all Hawkins' money
- ◆ the Mughal emperor had refused to grant special trading rights to the East India Company
- ◆ Hawkins had died on board his ship on the way back to England.

It was not a good start.

But within 150 years this same East India Company was making massive fortunes for its members and SHAREHOLDERS. Even more surprisingly, it ruled large parts of the Mughal emperor's lands across India. The men who had set out to become traders in India had become the rulers of India.

SOURCE 1 East India House, the London Headquarters of the East India Company. This engraving was made in 1784.

YOUR ENQUIRY

Your enquiry requires you to work out how and why, after such a poor start, the East India Company ended up as the virtual ruler of huge parts of India. The East India Company (at the time) and many British historians (since) claim that it was more or less an accident that the British ended up taking control of India. See what you think: were the British just traders who became 'accidental rulers' or did they know exactly what they were doing?

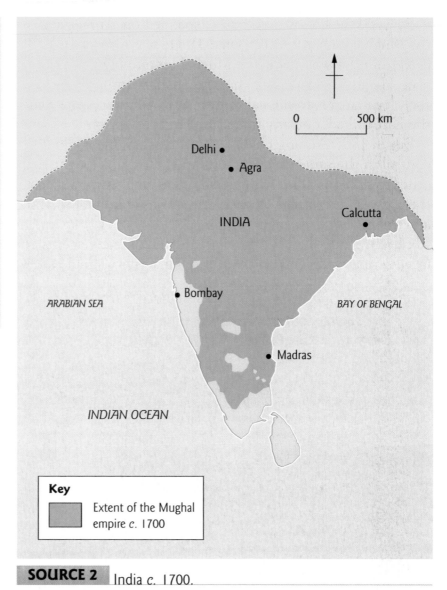

SOURCE 2 India c. 1700.

The EIC governors were not put off by the failure of Sir William Hawkins. They sent other representatives to India who won the right to set up small 'factories' as trading bases.

By 1700 the EIC owned land at three main bases in Madras, Bombay and Calcutta. From these bases, company agents would travel around trading with Indian merchants.

English travellers and traders in India were often impressed by what they saw. In 1679 Thomas Bowrey wrote about his travels in India and praised the country for its skilled craftsmen, able merchants, clever mathematicians, gifted artists and architects. He declared that the Indians were as intelligent as any people on Earth.

By 1700 the EIC had been trading in India for almost a century. From its scattered bases it had established a settled pattern of trade. It had won huge privileges: the merchants paid no taxes and no customs duties. The Company was very wealthy.

By 1700 the Company's trade depended on Aurangzeb, the Mughal emperor (see Source 3). He was a strict and powerful ruler who made the Mughal empire bigger than ever. He always made sure that the officials and princes in each local area stayed loyal to him. While Aurangzeb ruled, the East India Company traders had his protection.

But in 1707 Aurangzeb died. After this no one could keep control in the same way. His sons and grandsons fought each other to take his place while local rulers grabbed power for themselves and turned on each other in a scramble for land and riches.

Over the next half century East India Company agents faced serious problems, as the following activity should show.

SOURCE 3 An eighteenth-century portrait of Aurangzeb.

ACTIVITY

Soon you will play the East India Company Trading Game. But first you need some important information.

Each player takes the part of an East India Company agent. It is 1740. You are about to set off on an eight week journey through southern India, collecting the usual goods.

On your return (in other words when you have finished the game) you must write a report for the EIC directors in London. You must tell them:

◆ what sort of goods you have been trying to collect
◆ what helped you to trade (i.e. events from the game that made it easy to collect goods)
◆ what hindered your trade (i.e. events that made it difficult to collect goods)
◆ why you think the directors should take over areas of India and rule them. Explain why this will make trade easier ... but point out how it may cause some problems as well.

Good luck ... you may need it!

How to play the East India Company Trading Game

◆ Play the game in groups of three or four. Each player is a different agent.

◆ The game board is on pages 24–25. You will also need a dice, or six cards numbered one to six, shuffled and placed face down on the table.

◆ There will be eight rounds in the game. Each round represents one week.

◆ In each round you (and all the other players in turn) must:

1 roll the dice (or pick one of the cards)
2 find the correct number on the left-hand side of the board and look across to the correct week to find out what has happened to you
3 record what has happened in a journal, using a chart like the one below. Make sure you include enough details to help you write a really good report afterwards.

calico (cotton cloth)

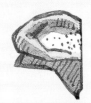
saltpetre
(for making gunpowder)

spices (e.g. pepper)

Week number	What happened	Goods gained or lost	Total crates so far

◆ When every player has finished Week 8 work out which agent in your group gathered the most crates. Did anyone reach 100?

Afterwards

When you have finished the game, work as a group to discuss what you could put in each of your reports to the East India Company directors. You will find that talking it through together makes it much easier to write a good report.

Use your journals (and the game board) to give you ideas about what made trade easier and what made trade harder.

Remember that your aim is to persuade the East India Company to take more control over large areas of India. Be sure to come up with lots of good reasons for doing this.

silk (for making clothes)

indigo (a type of dye)

precious gems

THE EAST INDIA COM

	week 1	week 2	week 3	week 4
1	War breaks out between rival princes. You cannot trade here.	You use EIC troops to fight for a local prince. He rewards you with 20 crates of silk.	War breaks out between rival princes. You cannot trade here.	French traders have bought all the goods from your regular contact here.
2	You bribe local officials to set up good trade links. You collect 15 crates of calico.	War breaks out between rival princes. You cannot trade here.	A Hindu festival is taking place here for many days. You move on, collecting nothing.	You bribe local officials to help you trade. Gain 15 crates of gems.
3	War breaks out between rival princes. You cannot trade here.	Local princes impose new taxes so you refuse to trade here.	One of your regular contacts has 20 crates of indigo for you.	A deadly disease is affecting this area. You leave straight away.
4	French traders have taken all the best goods here. You collect nothing.	You sign a treaty to support a local prince. He gives you 15 crates of spices.	One of your regular contacts has 15 crates of spices for you.	You admire a Hindu temple to please the local people. Gain 10 crates of silk.
5	You join in a Hindu festival. This pleases local traders. You gain 15 crates of spices.	This is a peaceful area. You trade easily and gain 30 crates of calico.	No one can control the bandits here. They take all the goods you have gained so far.	You sign a treaty to help a prince. You gain 20 crates of calico.
6	One of your regular merchant friends has 20 crates of indigo for you.	War breaks out between rival princes. You cannot trade here.	You use EIC troops to fight for a local prince. His reward is 20 crates of calico.	War breaks out between rival princes. You cannot trade here.

DANY TRADING GAME

week 5	week 6	week 7	week 8
You try to stop a local custom that you think is cruel. No one trades with you.	War breaks out between rival princes. You cannot trade here.	You sign a treaty to help a prince. He rewards you with 20 crates of spices.	War breaks out between rival princes. You cannot trade here.
You pay a high price to outbid rival French traders. Gain 10 crates of gems.	There has been a good harvest. You gain 20 crates of spices.	War breaks out between rival princes. You cannot trade here.	The monsoon season arrives early. You cannot trade in such heavy rain.
War breaks out between rival princes. You cannot trade here.	This is a very peaceful area. You gain 20 crates of indigo.	Landslides block the roads. You cannot trade in these conditions.	This is a peaceful area. You trade easily and gain 30 crates of calico.
You sign a treaty to support a local prince. You gain 20 crates of saltpetre.	War breaks out between rival princes. You cannot trade here.	There has been a good harvest. You gain 20 crates of spices.	Pirates capture the ship that was to collect your goods. You must stop trading.
One of your regular merchant friends has 20 crates of calico for you.	Local princes introduce new taxes so you refuse to trade here.	War breaks out between rival princes. You cannot trade here.	You use EIC troops to fight for a local prince. He gives you 30 crates of spices.
French traders have bought all the goods from your regular contact here.	EIC troops defeat local bandits. You gain 30 crates of calico.	War breaks out between rival princes. You cannot trade here.	You die of cholera ... but only after you have written your report!

3

EMPIRE BUILDERS: WHAT DO WE THINK OF WOLFE AND CLIVE?

Reach your judgement on these 'heroes of empire'

In the middle of the eighteenth century, Britain and France were the greatest nations on Earth. They had spread their power far beyond Europe in search of trade and wealth. They were rivals in America, India, the Caribbean and at sea all over the globe. In 1756, after years of squabbling, they went to war. It was a war that changed the world.

SOURCE I A painting of a sea battle between British and French ships during the Seven Years War.

By 1763 Britain emerged victorious from this 'Seven Years War'. Her success laid the foundations for her world-wide empire. It is not surprising, therefore, that two men whose victories turned the war in Britain's favour became heroes in their homeland. The names of James Wolfe and Robert Clive have been passed down through history as two of Britain's most remarkable empire builders. Source 2 shows how young people were once taught to admire such heroes.

SOURCE 2 An extract from a school history textbook published in 1956.

Every age has its heroes who stir the imagination and shape the lives of ordinary people. For the child in particular, tales of heroism and adventure, of high courage and achievement, are an important and essential part of his development, as well as his first introduction to history.

When we make a hero of someone, we sometimes say we are 'putting them on a pedestal'. A pedestal is a tall column on which statues are placed so that we literally look up to them.

In this enquiry we want you to learn about Wolfe and Clive and decide which of them you would put on a pedestal. Who is the greater hero? Or will you decide to leave the pedestal empty?

To make your decision, you will need to consider each man's story.

◆ You will need to work in two groups.

◆ When you study the life of Wolfe, Group 1 will gather evidence of reasons to show that Wolfe is a hero of the Empire who deserves to be put on the pedestal. Group 2 will do the opposite and try to show why Wolfe does not deserve to be called a hero.

◆ When you study the life of Clive, the roles will be reversed: Group 2 will find reasons to put Clive on the hero's pedestal; Group 1 will find reasons to oppose this.

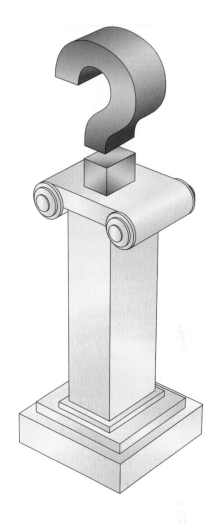

We begin by studying the story of General James Wolfe. In the following section, we deliberately tell the story of Wolfe's attack on Quebec in a way that makes him seem heroic. This should help Group 1. We have also included details of other factors that helped Wolfe. Group 2 could use these to show that heroes need help to make history!

◆ James Wolfe

SOURCE 3 Portrait of Wolfe painted in the 1760s.

Profile

- ◆ Born in Kent in 1727
- ◆ As a young boy Wolfe dreamed of being a great general
- ◆ He was tall, thin and pale with blue eyes and red hair
- ◆ He studied hard, doing extra lessons in subjects he thought would help him become a great general
- ◆ By sixteen he was already an army captain
- ◆ He impressed other officers with his bravery, but took many risks
- ◆ When he was 32 he led the British attack on French armies in North America
- ◆ At 33 he died just after capturing Quebec – the main French base in North America

DISCUSS A

1 Do you think that Wolfe looks like a hero in Source 3?
2 Which three facts from the profile of Wolfe's life would you be sure to use if you wanted to make him appear heroic?
3 Are there any facts that you would definitely leave out?

Rivalry in America

After a false start during Queen Elizabeth's reign, Britain had been able to set up thirteen valuable colonies on the east coast of North America. France had done something similar but, as Source 4 shows, her land ran to the north and west of the thirteen British colonies.

In 1758, during the Seven Years War, the British Prime Minister, William Pitt, decided to try to take Canada from the French. He knew that the key to Canada was the city of Quebec on the St Lawrence River. If the British held Quebec they could stop any supplies coming down the river and the French would have to surrender. The whole war might depend on this one mission. When choosing the man to lead the British against Quebec, Prime Minister Pitt took a risk: he ignored several older officers and turned instead to General James Wolfe.

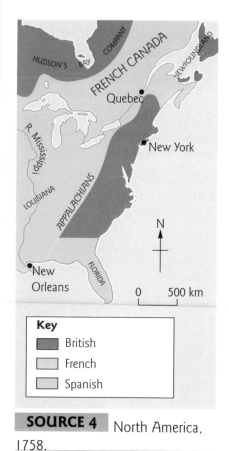

Key

- British
- French
- Spanish

SOURCE 4 North America, 1758.

Mission impossible – the attack on Quebec

The Prime Minister gave Wolfe a force of 8500 men. Wolfe trained the men very hard. He dismissed any soldiers who seemed unfit even though this cut down the size of his army.

In June 1759 the fleet set sail from Britain to Canada. The British ships went further down the narrow, shallow sections of the St Lawrence River than anyone else had ever managed. The navigator was James Cook, who later became another hero of the Empire (but that is another story). Without the navy, Wolfe could not have taken Quebec.

Outnumbered

Quebec stood high above the St Lawrence River. French guns to the east could smash any open attack from across the river, and to the south-west the city was protected by massive cliffs that no army could be expected to climb. The French army was twice the size of the British force. Many generals would have feared that they were doomed to fail. Wolfe did not let that thought cross his mind.

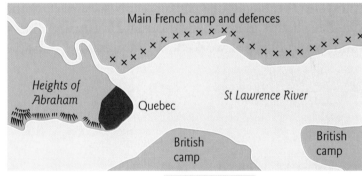

SOURCE 5 Quebec and its defences.

Wolfe ordered British ARTILLERY to pound the city. Quebec suffered terribly – but the French still controlled the river. A French officer sent a mocking message to Wolfe saying, 'You may destroy the town, but you will never get inside it'. Wolfe replied: 'I will take Quebec, even if I must stay until November'.

But time was Wolfe's enemy. The St Lawrence River would turn to ice long before November. Wolfe knew that he had to take Quebec within the next few weeks or his men would freeze to death, trapped in the bitter Canadian winter.

DISCUSS B

What reasons did the French have for thinking Quebec could never be taken?

The Heights of Abraham

Weeks passed and every attack by Wolfe failed. His army was cut to below 7000 by deaths, wounds and sickness. Wolfe himself was very unwell but he told the doctor, 'Patch me up for the work in hand. After that, nothing matters'.

Wolfe's officers wanted to land troops 13 kilometres up the river to the west and to march overland to attack the city. Wolfe finally agreed to attack from the west but invented a more sudden and daring approach: he was going to take 4000 men, at night, up the huge cliffs to the south-west of Quebec. If this plan failed, thousands of his men would die. If it worked, Wolfe would have done his duty for king and country and the British Empire in America would be safe.

On the night of 12 September, Wolfe silently launched his attack. Ships quietly carried 4000 men along the river towards Quebec. Wolfe read his favourite poem to the men as the ships closed in on their landing point.

The ships stopped where Wolfe had spotted a steep, narrow path that zigzagged 60 metres up the cliff face. Wolfe sent an advance party of 150 men up the dangerous path to deal with any French guards. He was lucky: the French officer in charge of guarding the cliffs had sent many of his men away to help with harvesting on nearby farms!

Just before dawn Wolfe's men reached the top of the cliffs and easily overwhelmed the shocked French guards who remained. By 6a.m. Wolfe's full force of 4000 men was in position on the Plains of Abraham above the cliffs. Quebec was barely 2 kilometres away.

As soon as he noticed that Wolfe's men had crossed the river, the French general, Montcalm, managed to gather about 9000 of his men to the Plains of Abraham. At ten o'clock, he ordered them to advance.

Wolfe told his men not to fire until the French were only about 36 metres away. They trusted him and did as he said. They kept their discipline and waited, ignoring the shots from the French. Finally, Wolfe gave the order to fire. The British guns unleashed such a burst of gunfire that the French later described it as being like a blast from a cannon. The British reloaded and fired again. The French were cut to pieces. The British tore into them with bayonets and swords, forcing them to turn and flee.

SOURCE 6 An engraving made in 1759, showing Wolfe's troops climbing the cliffs. Notice that the scale is wrong and that the attack is happening in daylight. Why do you think the artist has done this?

In the early moments of the battle, Wolfe was shot in the wrist but hid his injury with a handkerchief. Then he was hit in the groin by a piece of SHRAPNEL, and finally another bullet hit him in the chest and passed through both his lungs. An officer who was with him described what happened next:

SOURCE 7

'Support me,' cried Wolfe, 'lest my gallant soldiers should see me fall'. But he sank to the ground. He heard a British officer calling out, 'They run! See how they run!'
'Who run?' asked Wolfe.
'The enemy, sir. They give way everywhere!'
Wolfe now knew for certain that Quebec had fallen to the British. He turned on his side and exclaimed, 'God be praised! I now die in peace'.

D I S C U S S

Source 8 shows the death of General James Wolfe.
1 Which figure in the painting is James Wolfe?
2 How is Wolfe made to seem heroic in the painting?

SOURCE 8 *The Death of General Wolfe* painted by Benjamin West in 1770.

Consequences of Wolfe's victory

Although it cost him his life, Wolfe's victory at Quebec saved Britain's colonies in North America from falling into French hands. But the story has a twist to it. Things in history are never straightforward!

When the Seven Years War ended in 1763 France gave Canada and other land to the British (see Source 9). At first most people in Britain's Thirteen Colonies were delighted. They hoped to move west and take new land there. But the British government in London said they were not allowed to do this. The government was scared that colonists moving west might start expensive wars with the Native Americans who lived there. To make matters worse, the British Parliament started putting extra taxes on the Thirteen Colonies as a way of paying off some of the huge cost of the war.

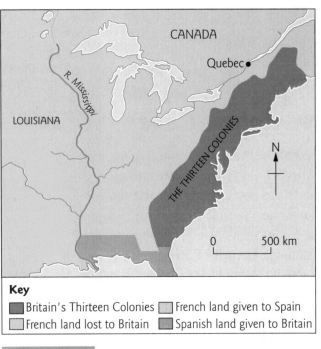

SOURCE 9 North America, 1763.

Key

■ Britain's Thirteen Colonies □ French land given to Spain
□ French land lost to Britain ■ Spanish land given to Britain

SOURCE 10 This is what the American flag looked like at the time of the War of Independence.

The colonists were furious! Their anger with the government grew until, in 1776, they finally issued their famous 'Declaration of Independence', saying that London no longer controlled them.

By 1783 the colonists had beaten Britain in a war and the Thirteen Colonies left the British Empire. They gave themselves a new name – The United States of America. Perhaps if Wolfe had failed to take Quebec, the British would never have owned Canada but their empire might have included all the land now owned by the USA. We will never know.

ACTIVITY

Look back through the story of empire builder General James Wolfe (pages 28–33). Group 1 should make a list of reasons to say why Wolfe DOES deserve to be called a hero. Group 2 should make a list of reasons to say why Wolfe DOES NOT deserve to be called a hero.

Now hold a class debate arguing for and against calling Wolfe a hero.

It is time to study our second empire builder as we learn about the extraordinary career of Robert Clive.

◆ Robert Clive

In this section, we tell Clive's story in a way that makes him seem heroic, exactly as we did for James Wolfe. This should help Group 2. We have also included details of other factors that helped Clive and we have shown aspects of his character that are not very appealing! Group 1 could use these to show that heroes need help to make history and that we may not want to put them on a pedestal when we look closely at their character.

SOURCE 11 A portrait of Robert Clive painted in 1770.

Profile

- ◆ Born in Shropshire in 1725
- ◆ As a boy, he was constantly picking fights
- ◆ Local shopkeepers paid Clive to stop him breaking their windows
- ◆ In 1743 Clive's father sent him to India to work for the East India Company (EIC)
- ◆ When the French threatened British trade in India, Clive joined the EIC army and quickly became a general
- ◆ From 1751 Clive won remarkable victories against much larger French and Indian armies
- ◆ After Clive's victories, Indian princes traded with the British and ignored the French
- ◆ In 1757 Clive's army of 3000 men won the Battle of Plassey against 60,000 Indians. He took all the riches of Bengal for the EIC
- ◆ After returning to England, in 1760 Clive became a Member of Parliament and then was made a lord

- ◆ In 1765 he returned to India as the EIC Governor of Calcutta
- ◆ In 1766 Clive went back to England with a fortune of over £3 million. His enemies accused him of corruption (accepting bribes)
- ◆ In 1772–73 Parliament investigated Clive's career and found him not guilty of corruption
- ◆ In 1774 Clive, who was depressed and addicted to opium, committed suicide

D I S C U S S A

1 Do you think Robert Clive looks like a hero in Source 11?
2 Which three facts from the profile of Clive's life would you be sure to use if you wanted to make him appear heroic?
3 Are there any facts that you would definitely leave out?

The man of action

As you read in Chapter 2, a group of English merchants started the East India Company in 1600. After a slow start, the Company set up three trading bases at Bombay, Madras and Calcutta.

At first the Company was not interested in taking over any land. Chapter 2 showed you why this changed. In 1707, the death of the Mughal emperor, Aurangzeb, led to a power vacuum. Wars broke out between rival princes. French traders helped the princes win battles and in return the princes promised to trade with the French. Unless the Company did something to stop this, it would be squeezed out of India.

In 1750 British trade in India seemed to be doomed. The French and the Indian princes they supported were on the verge of complete victory. Then Robert Clive entered the story. Just a few years before, he had been so bored with his office work for the East India Company that he had tried to commit suicide, but his gun failed to fire – twice! Only when

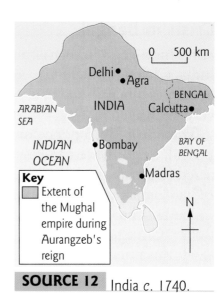

SOURCE 12 India c. 1740.

he joined the Company's army could he show his talents as a man of action.

In 1751 Clive led a force of 500 British and Indian soldiers and captured an important city called Arcot. He held the city for 50 days against a French and Indian army of 10,000 men. This gave the British time to recover. Over the next four years French power in southern India collapsed. The East India Company emerged as the closest friend and most favoured trading partner of the victorious princes.

DISCUSS B

Look at Source 13. How has the artist made Clive seem heroic in this picture?

SOURCE 13 An artist's reconstruction of Robert Clive at Arcot, from a school history textbook published in 1956.

Crisis in Bengal

After his success in southern India, Clive returned to Britain as a hero – and as a very wealthy man.

Then, in 1756, a prince in Bengal, in north-west India, dared to attack the East India Company's base in Calcutta. The Company sent Robert Clive to Bengal to teach this prince a lesson.

SOURCE 14 Siraj ud Dowlah, the Indian prince who attacked Calcutta in 1756.

Siraj ud Dowlah had become the nawab (prince) of Bengal early in 1756. He disliked the British taking a bigger and bigger part in his country's trade. Then the British, with their possessions under attack elsewhere in India, fortified their base in Calcutta. This was the last straw for the nawab. He didn't want other nations building forts in his own land. He feared the British were aiming to take over Bengal so he attacked Calcutta.

The story of the 'Black Hole of Calcutta'

When Siraj ud Dowlah attacked the East India Company base in Calcutta, his soldiers held a number of British men and women prisoner overnight, in a room that was about 5 metres by 4 metres with just two small windows.

SOURCE 15 One survivor, John Holwell, later wrote about his experiences:

Of 146 prisoners, 123 were smothered in the Black Hole prison in the night of 20 June 1756 ... From about nine till near eleven ... my legs were almost broke with the weight against them. I travelled over the dead and went to the other end of the room.

Many historians now think that John Holwell greatly exaggerated what happened and some say the event never happened at all. When Robert Clive reached Bengal in 1757, however, he certainly believed all he had been told about the 'Black Hole of Calcutta' and was determined to take full revenge on Siraj ud Dowlah. Clive knew this could be difficult and that he would be heavily outnumbered.

Here is another extract from the school history book from 1956 that started this enquiry. It tells the story of what happened when Clive finally met Siraj ud Dowlah at the Battle of Plassey on 23 June 1757.

SOURCE 16 From *People in History, No. 4, Great People of Modern Times*, by R.J. Unstead.

Clive's army consisted of only about 3000 men while Dowlah faced him with about 60,000. At first Clive decided that it was madness to risk a battle and he must retreat as most of his officers advised. By the next morning however, he had changed his mind and gave the order to advance. The great enemy army broke ranks and fled almost as soon as he attacked, so that the Battle of Plassey, 1757, was one of the most dazzling victories in the history of the world. The British became masters of Bengal, a province larger than the whole of Great Britain.

R.J. Unstead's book certainly makes Clive seem like a hero. See what you think as you look at a few more facts about the battle, and about what Clive had been doing before it started:

- ▲ Clive's troops were very well trained

- ▲ The nawab's troops were very disorganised

- ▲ Clive's army had eight modern six-pounder guns

- ▲ The nawab's army had 50 heavy cannon

- ▲ Clive chose a good battleground, giving some cover for his men

- ▲ Clive used his six-pounder guns well and destroyed the nawab's cannon

- ▲ Many of the nawab's richest subjects did not like him so Clive plotted with them before the battle. He told them to contact Mir Jafar who was one of the nawab's generals. Clive promised Jafar that he would be made the new ruler of Bengal if he supported the British

- ▲ When the battle started, Mir Jafar was still with the nawab's army – but he changed sides at the very last minute!

- ▲ During the battle a violent rainstorm soaked the nawab's ammunition supplies

- ▲ One of Clive's officers disobeyed him and gave the order to attack at just the right time to turn the battle Clive's way

- ▲ A lucky shot from a British gun killed the nawab's greatest general

- ▲ The nawab lost 500 men in the battle. Clive lost 18 men

The painting in Source 17 was made in 1761. By that time Clive had rewarded Mir Jafar by making him the new nawab of Bengal – but the EIC really controlled his lands.

SOURCE 17 Robert Clive meets Mir Jafar after the Battle of Plassey. A painting by Francis Hayman in 1761.

Discuss

Look at Source 17.

1 Why do you think the artist has shown both men in the picture?

2 How does the artist suggest that Clive and Britain are more important than Mir Jafar?

3 Some people say this painting looks more like a business deal than a battlefield. What might suggest this?

Consequences of Clive's victory

The Battle of Plassey in 1757 changed the history of the world. Mir Jafar became the new ruler of Bengal, but the East India Company held the real power over the richest area in India. Looking back, we can see that this was the start of the British Empire in India.

Over the next twenty years the Company became more closely involved in Indian politics. In 1765 Clive took over all tax collection in Bengal on behalf of the Company. He – and others – made enormous fortunes in India by bribery, deceit and threats. He said that this was what powerful Indians did and that it was natural that he should follow their example.

Back in Britain, Parliament and the public were ashamed of Clive. In 1772 he was put on trial for corruption. Even though he was not found to be guilty, his reputation never recovered. He became depressed, took drugs and finally killed himself in 1774.

ACTIVITY

Look back through the story of empire builder Robert Clive (pages 34–38). Group 2 should make a list of reasons to say why Clive DOES deserve to be called a hero. Group 1 should make a list of reasons why Clive DOES NOT deserve to be called a hero.

Now hold a class debate arguing for and against calling Clive a hero.

FINAL ACTIVITY

It is time to make up your own mind. Forget about being in Group 1 or Group 2. What do YOU think? Who should go on the pedestal? Should it be:

a) James Wolfe
b) Robert Clive
c) no one?

Whatever you decide you must use facts from the lives of these two extraordinary empire builders to support your case.

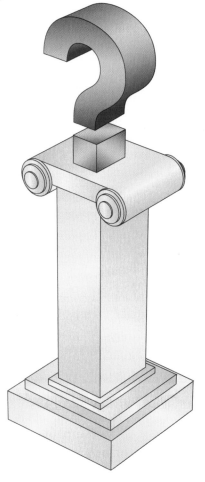

4

EMPIRE AND SLAVERY: HOW CAN WE TELL THE STORY OF BRITAIN'S SLAVE TRADE?

Use the evidence to tell two different versions of the slave trade

SOURCE 1 *The Slave Trade*, a painting by Francois Biard, 1840.

This painting shows a scene on the coast of West Africa in the early nineteenth century. It tells a disturbing story. If you look carefully you will find some shocking details of human misery and suffering.

DISCUSS

What details of human misery and suffering has the artist included in the painting in Source 1?

The people in the picture in Source 1 were caught up in one of the most shameful aspects of Britain's colonial history – the slave trade. For over three hundred years European countries forced Africans onto slave ships and transported them across the Atlantic Ocean. The slaves were then worked to death on plantations in North and South America, growing sugar, tobacco and cotton for Europe.

This is part of what is sometimes called 'the triangular trade'.

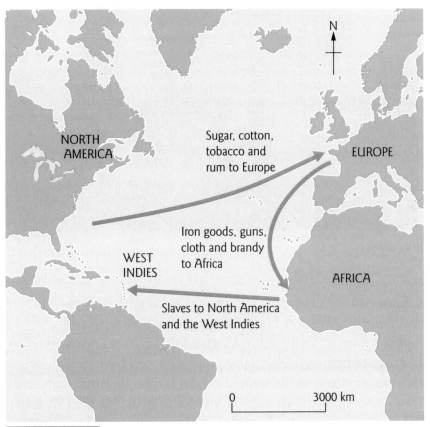

SOURCE 2 The triangular trade.

Europeans did not begin slavery in Africa. For thousands of years slavery had been part of African culture. But the European slave trade was on a different scale. Between 1500 and 1850 more than 11 million Africans arrived on European-owned plantations. Millions more (no-one knows the exact figure) died on the journey from their homes to the African coast or on the slave ships as they crossed the Atlantic.

The Portuguese were the first Europeans to trade in African slaves, but other European countries quickly joined in. By the eighteenth century the British were the main slave traders. As the demand for sugar in Britain grew, more and more Africans were taken to the West Indies to work on British sugar plantations.

YOUR ENQUIRY

Slavery is a disturbing part of British history. Many people today are shocked that Britain could have been involved in such a cruel trade. Some people would prefer to forget it completely. However, good historians do not ignore the difficult bits of the past. In this enquiry you will find out about Britain's slave trade and think about the best way to tell this shocking story.

◆ The journey of the Duke of Argyle

On a rainy August day in 1750 an old and shabby ship called the *Duke of Argyle* set sail from the port of Liverpool. John Newton, the ship's captain, was starting a fourteen-month journey which would take him to Africa, the West Indies and back to Britain.

Eight weeks after leaving Liverpool, with the West African coast in sight, the crew began to prepare the ship for its cargo – slaves.

For the next six months the *Duke of Argyle* sailed up and down the West African coast, slowly filling its holds with slaves. It worked like this: African traders kidnapped people from villages up to hundreds of kilometres inland. They marched them to the coast where European slave merchants like John Newton bought the slaves. As demand for slaves grew some African kings fought wars against other tribes in order to supply the African traders and the European demand.

By the end of May 1751 the *Duke of Argyle* was packed with slaves. As the ship left Africa for the West Indies, John Newton thought fondly of his wife in England:

SOURCE 3   An eighteenth-century painting of a slave ship.

SOURCE 4   An extract from John Newton's journal.

I have lost sight of Africa. It is now ten in the evening. I am going to walk the deck and think of you and, according to my constant custom, recommend you to the care and protection of God.

It seems strange to us today that a man like John Newton, who loved his wife and believed in God, could have been involved in a trade that caused so much human suffering. As he walked on deck that evening, hundreds of Africans were chained and stacked in the dark and airless holds below his feet. These people had lost their freedom and had been forced from their homeland. Many would never see their families again.

Conditions on slave ships like the *Duke of Argyle* were appalling. The slaves were stacked on shelves sometimes less than a metre apart. They were chained in twos at their hands and feet, making it difficult to move or turn without hurting themselves. When the weather was good the slaves were herded on deck for feeding. In bad weather they were fed below in their filthy quarters. A shared bucket was used as a toilet and this often overflowed in the Atlantic storms. The stink of the slave quarters was unbearable.

It is not surprising that in these conditions large numbers of slaves became sick. The biggest killer was DYSENTERY. This illness was nick-named 'the bloody flux'. Soon after the *Duke of Argyle* left Africa, John Newton began to record the deaths of slaves:

SOURCE 5 An extract from John Newton's journal.

Thursday 23 May ... Buried a man slave (No. 34).
Wednesday 29 May ... Buried a boy slave (No. 86) of a flux.
Wednesday 12 June ... Buried a man slave (No. 84) of a flux, which he had been struggling with near seven weeks.
Thursday 13 June ... This morning buried a woman slave (No. 47). Know not what she died of for she has not been properly alive since she first came on board.

In the 42 days that it took the miserable ship to cross the Atlantic a total of ten slaves died. Their bodies were thrown to the sharks.

The physical and mental suffering of the Atlantic crossing led many Africans into despair. Some became so depressed that they killed themselves by refusing to eat or by jumping overboard if they had the chance. Others were determined to resist.

Just three days into the voyage a young slave, who had been released from his chains because of sickness, managed to push a metal spike through the deck gratings to the slaves below. Within an hour twenty slaves were free. But the sailors had guns and were soon able to regain control. Few slave revolts were successful, but they were common.

At the beginning of July the *Duke of Argyle* approached the West Indies. The crew began to prepare the slaves for arrival. The Africans were taken on deck to be washed. Their holds were cleaned out. This was a likely time for a rebellion so they were exercised in small groups.

On 3 July the ship landed in Antigua. Many of the slaves were very ill. Some died soon after arrival. Those who survived were sold at auction to the highest bidder and taken away to one of the British sugar plantations.

Over the next six weeks John Newton loaded his ship with sugar and headed for home to his wife and family in Liverpool.

ACTIVITY

1 Which of these words would you use to describe John Newton from the evidence on these two pages: cruel, gentle, thoughtful, loving, honest, ruthless, unhappy?

2 We have focused on John Newton, but it took more than just a slave ship captain to make the slave trade work. Make a list of all the other people mentioned on these two pages. Describe their role in running the slave trade.

And ...

Our aim is to try to give people a rounded and truthful picture of the slave trade. Hidden in this account of John Newton's voyage are other interesting stories which we could have focused on:

Yes, why didn't you focus more on the slave rebellion? It shows that black people resisted slavery.

I think you should focus on Liverpool. Who was paying John Newton? It would show who was really behind the slave trade.

3 Read the account of John Newton's voyage again and then write two or three more speech bubbles each arguing for a different focus on Britain's slave trade.

◆ *Life on the sugar plantations*

The Africans whom John Newton took to the West Indies were bought by British planters. These men owned large sugar plantations on the islands. The planters made huge profits from the sugar trade and they lived in great luxury. On their plantations they not only grew the sugar cane, but also processed the sugar.

Sources 6–8 tell the story of sugar production on the West Indian plantations. Together they give us a very detailed picture of life on the plantations.

ACTIVITY

Look at Sources 6–8 very carefully and answer these questions:

1 What jobs did the following people do on the sugar plantations?

◆ Male slaves
◆ Female slaves
◆ Slave children
◆ White people

2 What made the work on the plantations so hard?
3 What do the pictures tell us about how the slaves were treated on the plantations?
4 These three paintings are by an artist who carefully observed what happened on the plantation. He was paid by the plantation owner who wanted the paintings to hang on the wall of his home in England. How does this affect your judgements in questions 1–3?

SOURCE 6 A print showing slaves working in the sugar cane fields, 1823.

SOURCE 7 A print showing slaves carting the sugar cane to the windmill to be crushed, 1823.

SOURCE 8 A print showing slaves working in the boiling house, 1823.

One problem with the pictures on pages 44–45 is that they all show the same plantation. So we need to ask ... how typical was this plantation?

The pictures show only one aspect of life on the plantation – work. So we need to ask ... what else happened? What aspects of a slave's life are missing?

Historians have tried to piece together a more detailed and accurate story of life on the sugar plantations using lots of different sources. Here are some of their findings:

1 The slaves usually worked from 6a.m. to 6p.m., six days a week. They had half an hour for breakfast and an hour and a quarter for midday break.

2 After arriving in the West Indies slaves could expect to live for only eight years.

3 Some African women worked in the plantation owners' houses as cooks, maids, nannies and washerwomen. This was better work than in the fields, but the hours were long and the women often had to cope with sexual harassment from the white men in the house.

4 Slaves were denied basic human rights. They were regarded as property which could be bought and sold.

5 Slaves suffered from tropical diseases such as YAWS, LEPROSY and dysentery. Sometimes they were able to use traditional African remedies to cure these diseases.

6 Slaves often made their work more bearable by singing African songs while they worked.

46

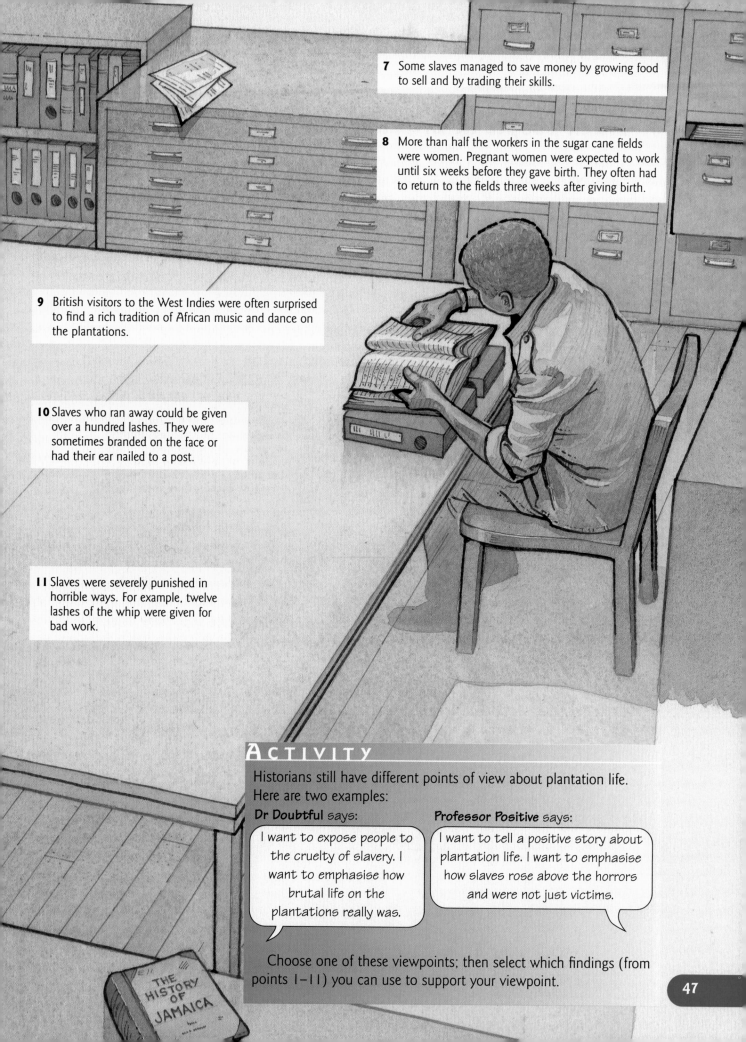

7 Some slaves managed to save money by growing food to sell and by trading their skills.

8 More than half the workers in the sugar cane fields were women. Pregnant women were expected to work until six weeks before they gave birth. They often had to return to the fields three weeks after giving birth.

9 British visitors to the West Indies were often surprised to find a rich tradition of African music and dance on the plantations.

10 Slaves who ran away could be given over a hundred lashes. They were sometimes branded on the face or had their ear nailed to a post.

11 Slaves were severely punished in horrible ways. For example, twelve lashes of the whip were given for bad work.

ACTIVITY

Historians still have different points of view about plantation life. Here are two examples:

Dr Doubtful says:

I want to expose people to the cruelty of slavery. I want to emphasise how brutal life on the plantations really was.

Professor Positive says:

I want to tell a positive story about plantation life. I want to emphasise how slaves rose above the horrors and were not just victims.

Choose one of these viewpoints; then select which findings (from points 1–11) you can use to support your viewpoint.

◆ *Black people in Britain*

One of the results of the slave trade was that more black people came to Britain. Africans had been in Britain since Roman times, but it was in the eighteenth century that black people settled in Britain in large numbers. Some were slaves brought to Britain by their masters. Others were former slaves who had been granted their freedom or who had escaped from the plantations.

It is difficult to write about the history of black people in Britain in the eighteenth century because few left a record of their experiences. However, if we search in the sources that we have and think hard, we can begin to tell the stories of Britain's early black communities.

ACTIVITY A

In this activity the action shifts to Britain. But again, our two historians want to tell rather different stories:

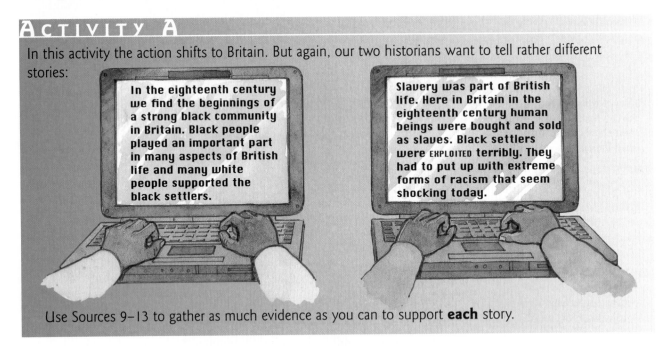

> In the eighteenth century we find the beginnings of a strong black community in Britain. Black people played an important part in many aspects of British life and many white people supported the black settlers.

> Slavery was part of British life. Here in Britain in the eighteenth century human beings were bought and sold as slaves. Black settlers were EXPLOITED terribly. They had to put up with extreme forms of racism that seem shocking today.

Use Sources 9–13 to gather as much evidence as you can to support **each** story.

SOURCE 9 A painting of the family of Sir William Young painted in 1766. The black servant in the picture is a groom. In other rich households black people worked as gardeners, footmen and maids. During the eighteenth century it became fashionable to include a black servant in family portraits. This was a way in which rich people showed off their wealth.

A fine Negro boy

offered for sale in Liverpool.

Is said to be about 4 ft 5 in. tall. Of a sober, tractable [willing], humane disposition. Eleven or twelve years of age, talks English very well, and can dress hair in a tolerable way.

SOURCE 10 This advertisement for a slave appeared in a Liverpool newspaper called *Williamson's London Advertiser* in 1768.

SOURCE 11 This advertisement for a runaway slave appeared in a London newspaper called the *Public Advertiser* in 1768. Many advertisements like this one appeared in newspapers during the eighteenth century.

Run away from his master, a Negro boy, under five feet in height, about 16 years old, named Charles. He is very ill made, being remarkably bow-legged, hollow-backed and pot-bellied. He had on, when he went away, a coarse dark brown linen coat, a thick waistcoat, very dirty leather breeches and on his head an old velvet cap.

Whoever will bring him, or give any news of him, to Mr Beckford in Pall Mall, will be handsomely rewarded.

SOURCE 12 In 1771, James Somerset, a black slave in London, escaped from his master Charles Stewart. Somerset went into hiding in London's black community, but his master found him, placed him in chains and tried to send him back to the West Indies. Somerset's friends managed to bring his case to court. The judge, Lord Mansfield, ordered Somerset to be freed because, although slavery was still legal in Britain, slaves could not be taken from Britain by force.

This report of the celebrations in the black community appeared in the *Public Advertiser* in June 1772:

On Monday near 200 Blacks, with their ladies, had an entertainment at a public house in Westminster, to celebrate the triumph which their brother Somerset had obtained over Mr Stewart, his master. Lord Mansfield's health was echoed round the room and the evening was concluded with a ball. The tickets for admittance to this black assembly were 5s each.

ACTIVITY B

Work in pairs. One of you is Professor Positive, one is Dr Doubtful. You are being interviewed for a TV programme about attitudes towards black people in Britain in the past.

Choose three of the sources on pages 48–49. For each of the sources you have chosen, explain how it supports your overall argument.

SOURCE 13 This is a portrait of Ignatius Sancho. It was painted in 1768 by Thomas Gainsborough, one of the leading artists of the time. Sancho was a famous black writer and musician who owned a shop in London. He was born on a slave ship heading for Grenada. While Sancho was still a small child his mother died and his father killed himself rather than be a slave. Sancho came to London as a child and eventually became butler to the Duke of Montague. Sancho soon taught himself to read and write. In 1773 he married Anne, a black woman, and opened a grocery shop in Westminster. Sancho had many friends among London's artistic community. His compilation of letters became a best-seller when it was published as a book in 1782.

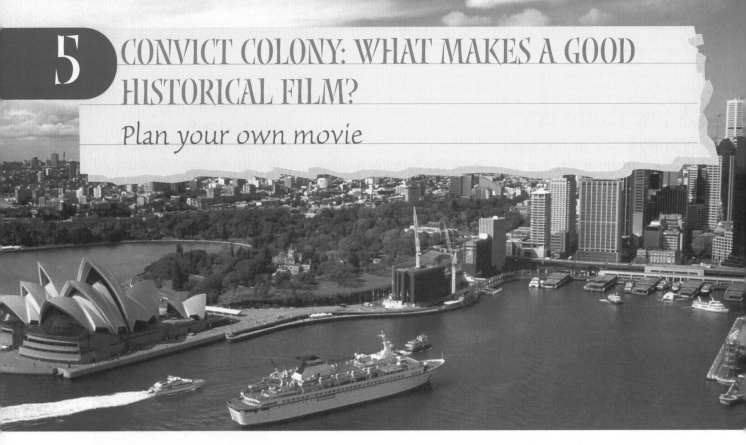

5 CONVICT COLONY: WHAT MAKES A GOOD HISTORICAL FILM?

Plan your own movie

You probably recognise this place – Sydney harbour, Australia. Even though Australia is on the other side of the world it is a country that seems very familiar to us. We speak the same language, play the same sports and watch some of the same television programmes. We might even have friends or relatives who live in Australia.

In the eighteenth century Europeans knew hardly anything about Australia. In 1770 Captain James Cook and his crew sailed their ship, the *Endeavour*, along part of the eastern coast of Australia, where Sydney now stands. Cook and his men were disappointed by the barren landscape. They collected some strange plants and creatures, but left after a few days. For seventeen years after Cook's voyage no other Europeans went to this vast, unknown land.

Then, in 1787, the British government made an extraordinary decision. For many years criminals had been transported across the seas as an alternative to being hanged or imprisoned in England. At first they were sent to America, where they were forced to work for plantation owners. But by 1787 America was no longer part of the British Empire, and English prisons had begun to overflow. The government decided to turn the newly discovered continent of Australia into a vast jail!

The man in Source 1 was chosen to lead the first convict fleet and to govern the new colony. His name was Captain Arthur Phillip. During the winter and spring of 1787 Phillip prepared for the voyage. He bought the eleven small ships that would make the long journey to Australia and organised all the other supplies that would be needed.

The first convicts arrived, chained together and shivering, in the open wagons that carried them to Portsmouth. Few of these people were dangerous criminals. James Grace, an eleven-year-old boy, had simply stolen some ribbon and a pair of silk stockings.

SOURCE 1 A portrait of Captain Arthur Phillip.

The convicts were herded on board the ships. Their quarters had no portholes, and candles were banned because of the risk of fire. By May 1787 nearly 1500 people – officers, seamen, marines and convicts – were crammed onto the ships. They then began the long and terrifying journey beyond the seas.

SOURCE 2 The route of the First Fleet's journey to Australia, 1787–88.

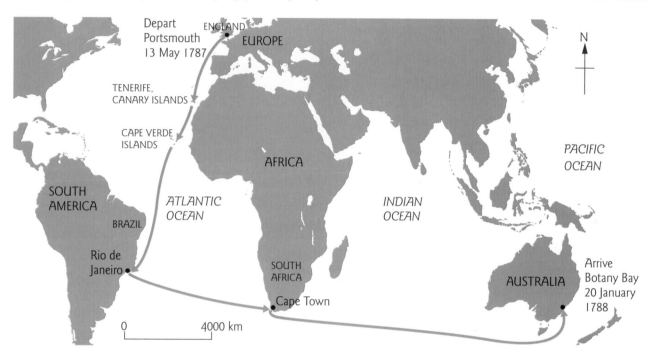

Source 2 shows the 24,000-kilometre journey that the First Fleet made to Australia. You can see that Phillip took an indirect route in order to pick up supplies and to take advantage of the winds and currents. At first the voyage went well, but in the tropics the crew and convicts were plagued with rats, bedbugs, lice, fleas and cockroaches. The BILGES sloshed with a mixture of urine, vomit, dung and dead rats.

After leaving Cape Town the convict quarters became more crowded than ever because the convicts had to make room for the farm animals which Phillip bought for the new colony. On 19 January 1788 the crew on Phillip's flagship, the *Sirius*, finally saw the coast of Australia – eight months after leaving England!

Phillip's fleet anchored in what would later become Sydney harbour. In his journal Phillip described it as 'the finest harbour in the world'. It was here, in the weeks that followed, that Britain's convict colony was built. Between the years 1787 and 1868 more than 160,000 convicts were transported from England and Ireland to Australia.

SOURCE 3 The *Sirius*, flagship of the First Fleet, at anchor in Sydney harbour.

YOUR ENQUIRY

In this enquiry you will make plans for a film about Britain's convict colony in Australia. You will need to use your imagination to select key events, interesting characters and exciting locations to keep viewers interested. You will also have to make sure that your film is as historically accurate as possible.

◆ The criminals

Thomas Holden was a weaver from Bolton, Lancashire. In 1812 he was involved in forming an early trade union to fight for the rights of weavers. For this 'crime' Thomas was sentenced to seven years transportation.

SOURCE 4 From his cell in Lancaster Castle, Holden wrote this letter to his wife, Molly:

Dear Wife,
It is with sorrow that I have to tell you that today, at my trial, I received the hard sentence of seven years transportation beyond the seas. If I was to be in prison I would try and content myself, but to be sent from my native country, perhaps never to see it again, distresses me beyond comprehension. To part with my dear wife and child, parents and friends, to be cut off in the bloom of my youth without doing any wrong to any person on earth – oh my hard fate! May God have mercy on me.
Your affectionate husband until death.
Thomas

SOURCE 5 An engraving of a convict hulk at Portsmouth, 1828.

Thomas Holden could not bear to be separated from his wife and child. Other letters have survived in which he pleaded with Molly to raise the money for her passage to Australia. She did not.

Thomas was soon taken from Lancaster Castle to the south coast of England. The journey lasted eight days. He travelled in an open cart with other men, women and children. The convicts were heavily chained and dressed in rags. They had no protection from the rain or from the taunts of the people they passed on the road.

For the next five months Thomas Holden was imprisoned on a hulk like the one you can see in Source 5. The hulks were old warships, left to rot and used as prisons in the ports of southern England. They were cramped, wet, dark and vile-smelling places. New convicts were forced to hand over all their possessions. A heavy iron was fastened to their right ankle. The convicts were then ready to work from dawn until dusk on the government dockyards. The hulks were brutal places. Even small children were placed in irons. Flogging was common. Female convicts were often raped.

◆ The voyage

By the 1820s most convict ships took about four months to reach Australia, making only one stop, at Rio de Janeiro in South America. Today, it is hard for us to imagine the suffering that people faced on such a long and difficult journey. About two hundred convicts were crammed into the holds of a converted merchant ship. Four convicts shared a wooden BERTH 2 metres square. There was less than 2 metres headroom. The only air came from the hatchways, which were covered with heavy iron grilles and were heavily padlocked. In the blazing heat of the tropics the PITCH melted and burned the convicts' flesh as it dripped from the timbers.

Once the ships were in open sea the convicts' leg-irons were removed. However, their bunks were fixed with irons so that they could be chained up if they misbehaved. For serious offences, such as mutiny, convicts would be brought on deck, tied to a grating and given 50 lashes with a CAT O' NINE TAILS. The prisoners and the ship's company watched the painful flogging in silence. It is not surprising that there were few mutinies on the convict ships.

The ship's surgeon tried to make sure that as many prisoners as possible survived the journey. He issued lime-juice each day to protect the convicts from SCURVY. Whenever possible, he brought the convicts on deck for fresh air and exercise. Convicts complained about the 'salted horse meat' which they were sometimes given to eat. In the tropical heat, two pints of warm, dirty water a day left the convicts thirsting for more. But at least the surgeon made sure that each person had enough food and water to stay alive. After 1815, only one convict in a hundred died on the voyage to Australia.

SOURCE 6 A nineteenth-century painting of a convict ship.

ACTIVITY

Use these headings to write the plan for the first part of your film, which will look at the transportation of the convicts to Australia.

Characters
Make Thomas Holden your main character, but decide on three or four other characters who will be introduced in the first part of your film. Use your background knowledge and imagination to write short character sketches about each of your characters. Make sure you explain how each character was involved in transportation.

Events and locations
Use your background knowledge and imagination to work out a sequence of five or six events and their locations, which will form the story in the first part of your film. For example, your first event and location might be:

Event	Location
Thomas Holden is sentenced to seven years transportation	The court room in Lancaster Castle

Historical accuracy
A really good film will need to be historically accurate. Make a list of up to five important ideas about the system of transportation which you want people to understand in the first part of your film.

In order to make your film really accurate there will be lots of questions about the system of transportation and daily life at that time which you will need to research. Make a list of these questions for your team of researchers.

◆ *The convict colony*

The second part of your film will cover Thomas Holden's life at the convict colony. The pictures and information in this section should give you lots of ideas about how your story might develop.

Source 7 shows a picture of Sydney harbour painted 33 years after the first convicts landed. You can see how much the area developed in that time.

SOURCE 7 A painting of Sydney harbour in 1821.

DISCUSS A

1 What does Source 7 tell us about life in the convict colony in 1821?
2 In what ways has the artist made Sydney seem a pleasant place to live?

On the left of the picture in Source 7 you can see a group of convicts quarrying stone. All the convicts who arrived in Sydney faced several years of hard labour. At night they were locked up in the convict barracks, but during the day they dug ditches, felled trees, planted crops, put up buildings and built roads. If they were lucky they might find themselves working as a labourer for one of the free settlers who had come to farm in the colony. All convicts were expected to work for ten hours a day from Monday to Friday and for six hours on Saturday. If they worked more hours than this they were paid for the extra work – either in money or in rum.

To the west of Sydney, in the distance, were the Blue Mountains. In 1813 three settlers found a way across this huge mountain range and were amazed by the rich, golden grassland on the other side. In the years that followed, difficult convicts were sent to build roads over the Blue Mountains. Life in a 'road gang' like the one in Source 8 was terrible. Day after day convicts broke stones and shovelled earth with heavy irons biting into their legs. They spent the freezing nights in prison huts on wheels, which they dragged behind them as the road was made.

SOURCE 8 A road gang on the Great West Road across the Blue Mountains, painted by Augustus Earle, 1826.

DISCUSS B

1 What does Source 8 tell us about the road gangs?
2 What aspects of life in a road gang are not shown in this picture?

Britain's PENAL colony in Australia was based on harsh punishment. Source 9 shows one of the most common forms of punishment – flogging. Convicts who broke the colony's rules were given 25, 50 or as many as 100 lashes. Even 25 lashes was a terrible torture which skinned a man's back and left it a tangled web of knotted scars. Men who were able to stand up to a flogging in silence were known as 'pebbles' or 'iron men'. A man who cried and screamed was called a 'sandstone' because he was said to crumble like the rock around Sydney harbour. There were always more 'sandstones' than 'pebbles'.

SOURCE 9 An engraving of a convict being flogged. 1836.

SOURCE 10 The first Australian railway, painted c. 1840.

Source 10 shows the first version of a railway in the convict colony. As you can see, it was powered by male convicts. Obviously, these men could not be kept in leg irons and this made it quite easy for a convict to escape. Escaping was easy; the hard thing was to survive. Some convicts took to the sea in stolen boats or on home-made rafts. A lucky few might be picked up by a merchant ship in need of more crew, but most drowned.

Other convicts, kown as 'bushrangers', ran off into the BUSH. They kept themselves alive by catching wild animals or by stealing from travellers and Aborigines. Few escaped convicts survived for very long in the harsh environment of the Australian bush.

The place that convicts feared more than any other was Van Diemen's Land – the island, now called Tasmania, which lies to the south of Australia.

Macquarie Harbour, Van Diemen's Land, was the wettest and most windswept place in Australia. The ferocious sea made escape impossible. It was here that the most troublesome convicts were sent. They lived in the cold barracks on Sarah Island, off the coast of Van Diemen's Land. At 6a.m. each morning they were herded onto boats and taken to the mainland to cut down the huge pine trees in the forests around the harbour. The convicts at Macquarie Harbour worked twelve hours a day in winter and sixteen hours in summer. Most of the time they were half-starved and chilled to the bone. If they broke an axe or insulted a guard, they were taken to Grummet Island. No convict could land here without being soaked, so they had to sleep naked or in wet clothes, without a fire or a blanket.

Source 11 shows convicts towing a raft of pine logs to the sawmill at Sarah Island. To the right is Grummet Island with the punishment hut. You can see the dark opening in the rock where prisoners who misbehaved were kept in solitary confinement.

SOURCE 11 A sketch of Macquarie Harbour, Van Diemen's Land, by T.J. Lempriere, 1830.

ACTIVITY

You now need to plan the second part of your film based on Thomas Holden's life in the convict colony.

Characters
Write brief character sketches for three or four new characters who will appear in the second part of your film.

Events and location
Use your background knowledge and imagination to work out a sequence of four or five events and locations that will form the story in the second part of your film.

Historical accuracy
◆ Make a list of up to five important ideas about the convict colony which you want people to understand in the second part of your film.
◆ Think of some good questions about life in the convict colony for your team of researchers.

◆ *The Aborigines*

From what you have read so far, you might think that Australia was an empty land when Britain set up the penal colony. Of course, this was not the case. When James Cook landed in Australia in 1770 the island was inhabited by around 300,000 native Australians – Aborigines. It is now time to bring the Aborigines into the plans for your film.

The Aborigines had lived in Australia for thousands of years before white people arrived on their shores. Aborigines live in hundreds of different tribes, each tribe sharing a particular language and occupying the territory where their ancestors lived. The area around Sydney was the ancestral home of the Iora tribe. The information on this page summarises the Iora's lifestyle and beliefs.

The Iora lived by the coast and their main diet was fish. The women of the tribe twisted fishing lines from pounded bark fibre and made hooks from shells. The Iora fished from canoes which they made from bark.

The Aborigines were not farmers. They did not plant crops or grow fruit and vegetables. Iora women gathered plants from the wild.

Too many children would have made it impossible for the Iora to move around and therefore to survive. A woman could only carry one child as well as food and implements. To avoid having large families the Iora caused abortions by giving pregnant women herbal medicines. If this failed they killed the unwanted child at birth.

Sometimes the men hunted animals on land using fire-sticks, stone axes and spears. They threw their spears with great accuracy and power. They had not invented the bow and arrow, but they were very skilful in tracking and stalking animals.

The Iora, like all Aborigines, were very spiritual people. They had no churches or temples. Instead, every hill, tree, stream and animal had spiritual meaning. The Iora did not believe that anyone could own the land, but if their territory was taken away it would mean a spiritual death.

The Iora never washed. They spent their lives coated in a mixture of fish oil, animal grease, sand, dust and sweat.

In order to survive, the tribe wandered easily over a wide area, feeding as they went. For this reason they could not have permanent houses. Instead, they lived in sandstone caves or in quickly-made bark shelters.

DISCUSS

Look at the information on this page carefully and then think of three reasons why some white people in the eighteenth century might have thought that the Aborigines were inferior people.

57

'Warra, warra!' These were the first words spoken by the Aborigines to the British in Australia. They mean 'go away'. But the British did not go away. When the First Fleet landed in 1788 two Iora tribesmen threw spears which landed wide of the white soldiers. One soldier fired a blank cartridge and the Iora ran away.

At first there was little violence between the white people and the Aborigines. Arthur Phillip gave strict orders that the Aborigines should not be harmed in any way. This continued to be the official policy of the British government in the years that followed.

The British government did not deliberately set out to kill the Aborigines. But the white settlement in Australia destroyed the Aborigines' way of life. Cholera and influenza germs from the convict ships soon infected the native Australians. Rum, which soldiers and convicts in the colony drank in huge amounts, ruined the lives of many Aborigines. On the shores around Sydney white people soon outnumbered Aborigines. The Iora began to die in huge numbers.

D I S C U S S

1 Explain what is happening in each of the pictures on the notice in Source 12.
2 What message did the governor want to give to the Aborigines?

SOURCE 12 A notice that the governor of the convict colony produced for the Aborigines in 1828.

From the very beginning of the colony, there was conflict between the convicts and the Aborigines. Convicts stole the Aborigines' weapons to sell as souvenirs. The white prisoners thought of the Aborigines as savages because they could not understand their way of life. They hated the fact that if a convict managed to escape it was often the Aborigines who tracked him down and returned him to the colonial authorities. The convicts came to see the Aborigines as pests who could be killed without hesitation.

As Britain's convict colony grew, kangaroos and other native animals were driven out to make room for sheep and cows. Fences blocked ancient routes. Forests were cut down. Native plants died out. In these ways the Aborigines' way of life was destroyed. The British government declared that all Australia belonged to the Crown. It argued that the Aborigines had no rights over the land because they simply wandered over it. This policy forced the Aborigines off their own land. By the 1830s Iora families, dressed in English rags and drunk on English rum, were a common sight around Sydney (see Source 13).

SOURCE 13 Aborigines on the edge of Sydney, from a painting by Augustus Earle, 1830.

ACTIVITY

You need to think of a way to include the Aborigines in your film. Look again at your ideas about characters, events and locations in the second part of your film. Write a paragraph to explain how you will build the Aborigines into your storyline.

◆ Make a list of five important ideas about the Aborigines which you want the audience to understand.

◆ Think of some good questions about the Aborigines for your team of researchers.

FINAL ACTIVITY

A Hollywood producer has decided he wants to make your film, but he needs to raise the money to pay for it. He wants you to make a trailer for the film to show to the 'money men'. Choose one scene from each of the three parts of the film that you have worked on (Transportation, The Convict Colony and The Aborigines). Briefly describe what should go into each scene so that it shows the most important features.

Draw a graph to show changing relationships in India

◆ The story of Thomas Coryate

This is Thomas Coryate. You have probably never heard of him. He is not very famous and he did little to change history (except that he was the man who introduced the fork to Britain's dining tables!). He is typical of many people or events from the past whose little-known stories often remain hidden from history books.

But Coryate did live a fascinating life. He was the son of a Somerset vicar and served for a while as a jester at the court of King James I. He then surprised everyone by setting off on long walking tours of Europe and beyond. In 1612 he set off on his final and longest journey – to India.

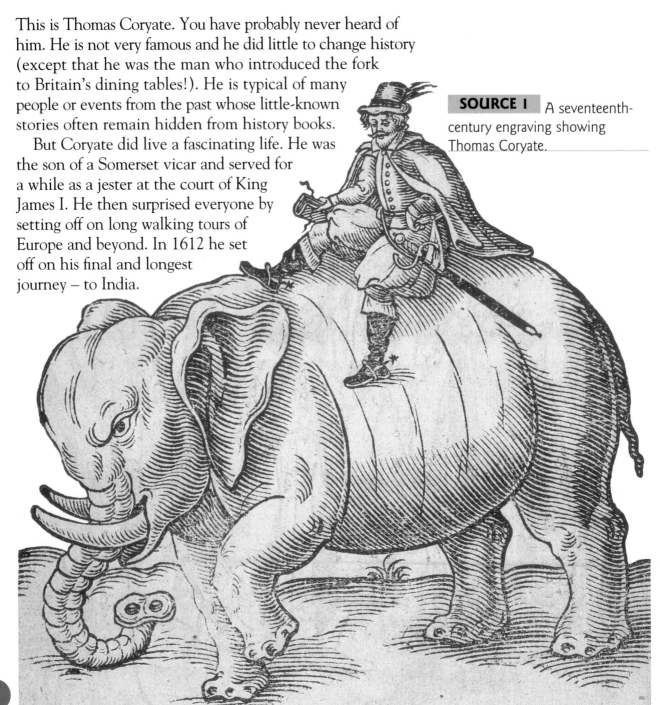

SOURCE 1 A seventeenth-century engraving showing Thomas Coryate.

When Coryate reached India in 1615, he visited the court of the mighty Mughal emperor, Jahangir. The emperor had recently allowed Englishmen to trade in his lands and so Coryate's arrival was not entirely surprising. The emperor was rather puzzled by his strange visitor but gave him a few minutes of his time, lent him some money and then ignored him. Even when Coryate preached Christianity from the MINARET of a mosque, the emperor did nothing. He – and many others – thought Coryate was slightly mad but harmless.

No one would pretend that Thomas Coryate was of great importance in history, but historians still love to find out about people like him. His story is fascinating in itself but it can also be used to sum up something far bigger. His odd ramblings through India can be used to sum up just how insignificant and harmless the British were to life in India at the start of the seventeenth century. As time went by, the Indians discovered that the British were to be anything but insignificant in the history of their country!

YOUR ENQUIRY

In this enquiry you will use little-known stories to sum up changes in the relationship between the British and the Indians between 1800 and 1897. In each case you will need to make a 'summary sheet' which tells the main points of the story very simply and makes clear what it shows about the bigger picture. (To help you, we have already done a summary sheet about Thomas Coryate's story as an example.) At the end of the enquiry you will take all your summaries and use them to make a display that tells the bigger story of a century of change.

The story of Thomas Coryate	What the story tells us
 Coryate was an Englishman who was a jester at the court of King James I of England. He travelled on foot around India in 1612. He found out about Indian customs and preached Christianity. The Indians thought he was mad.	Coryate's story symbolises the way in which the first British visitors to India seemed to pose no threat to the Indian way of life. The English just seemed a little odd and the Indians were prepared to welcome them to their country, and then ignore them for most of the time.

◆ *The story of the Prime Minister's granny*

Thomas Coryate may not have been famous or powerful but this man certainly was. This is Lord Liverpool. He lived 200 years later than Coryate and was the British Prime Minister from 1812 to 1827. History books mention many of his achievements, but there is one fact about him that very few textbooks include. If you read on you will find out about his 'hidden history' and what it symbolises about Britain's relationship with India.

SOURCE 2 A portrait of Lord Liverpool painted in 1827.

Britain's trade with India was just beginning when Thomas Coryate was alive. In the 200 years that followed, much changed. The British East India Company fought wars against Indian princes who made trade difficult. In 1757 General Robert Clive won the Battle of Plassey (see Chapter 3) which gave the British control over India's richest region, Bengal. More and more British traders, soldiers and officials settled in India.

Despite great differences between them, the British and the Indians generally mixed well together at first. Quite a few British traders and soldiers had wives or partners who were Indian. One British general was famous for parading around Calcutta with his thirteen Indian wives, each mounted on the back of a different elephant!

SOURCE 3 A rich and powerful East India Company trader called William Palmer. He is pictured with two of his Indian wives, three of his children and three other women. Palmer was of mixed Indian and British heritage. There were many such families in the trading cities of Calcutta, Madras and Bombay. This picture was painted in 1786.

DISCUSS A

What does Source 3 suggest about William Palmer's attitude towards his family?

One of the many Englishmen who mixed freely with the Indians in the eighteenth century was William Watts. He was an East India Company official who worked as a sort of secret agent before the Battle of Plassey in 1757. Acting on behalf of Robert Clive, Watts made a treaty with a powerful Indian prince called Mir Jafar. The deal was that Mir Jafar would not use his troops against the British in the battle. As a result, the British won the battle and conquered the rich province of Bengal. In return, the British gave Mir Jafar power over much of Bengal.

Watts lived in Calcutta and was married to an Indian woman. In 1750 they had a daughter, Amelia, who later married into the rich and powerful Jenkinson family. In 1812 Amelia's only son, Robert Jenkinson, became … you've guessed it: Lord Liverpool, Prime Minister of Britain. The surprising fact that in 1812 Britain had a Prime Minister who had an Indian granny is another little piece of 'hidden history'.

SOURCE 4 William Watts and Mir Jafar making the agreement.

DISCUSS B

Look back at the picture of Lord Liverpool on page 62. Can you see anything to suggest that his grandmother was Indian?

The story of Lord Liverpool's granny shows how close Britain and India had become by the end of the eighteenth century. They traded together, they made treaties, they married each other. Some British men even followed the Indian custom of having several wives. Neither the British nor the Indians objected. Each race seemed happy to accept the other's way of life despite their differences. But that was to change, as we will see.

ACTIVITY

Make a summary sheet about Lord Liverpool. Use the one on page 61 as an example. Make sure that your sheet has the main heading, *The story of the Prime Minister's granny*. In the first column sum up the main facts about Lord Liverpool – who he was, what his link was to India, etc. In column 2, explain what this piece of hidden history tells us about relationships between British people and Indians in the late eighteenth century.

◆ *The statue's story*

In 1997 the statue in Source 5 was set up in Bristol. It commemorates a remarkable man who died in the city in 1833. His story involves religion, superstition, determination and death. It is not well known, but it tells about a really significant change in the way the British ruled India in the early nineteenth century.

'Live and let live'

When the British first came to India they marvelled at its main religion, Hinduism. Over thousands of years the Indians had developed many religious customs and practices that must have seemed strange or alarming to the British.

Before 1800, British traders were happy to accept or ignore these customs no matter how odd they seemed. After all, they were East India Company merchants. They were traders, not rulers. It might have caused problems among the Indians they traded with if they had tried to interfere. On the whole they decided that it would be best to 'live and let live'. But around 1800 that attitude began to change.

SOURCE 5 Statue of Rammohan Roy on College Green, Bristol.

SOURCE 6 A portrait of William Carey.

Challenging the culture

The evangelicals were a powerful group of Christians. They took their Christian faith very seriously. They did not believe in 'live and let live'. They believed they should try to convert people of other faiths to Christianity.

One famous evangelical was William Carey. He was sure that God wanted him to go to India to convert people to Christianity. He arrived in Calcutta in 1793.

At first, British leaders in India – including some bishops – were angry that Carey had come to India. They were scared that he might upset Indian traders by interfering in Hindu beliefs. In fact, Carey won the respect of most Indians. Over the next 40 years, he treated them with great love and respect while challenging some of their customs.

Sati

In 1811 a deeply religious Indian called Rammohan Roy attended the funeral of his brother in West Bengal. Roy and his family were Hindus. The body was to be burned according to Hindu custom.

The body was carried forward. Then another figure appeared through the crowd. It was the dead man's widow. She was frightened – but she knew her duty. She allowed herself to be tied to her dead husband's corpse.

Roy begged his sister-in-law not to go through with this ancient Indian custom, but the other relatives forced him back. They believed her suicide would show her love for her husband – and would help to pay for any sins her husband had committed. Roy watched as the widow was placed on the bonfire alongside her husband's dead body. She choked and screamed as the smoke and flames enveloped her. She burned alive. The relatives danced around the fire singing 'Maha sati! Maha sati!' (A great wife! A great wife!)

From that day on Roy made up his mind to end this Hindu custom of widow burning, or 'sati' as it was known. He knew that very few of his fellow Indians would help him. He also knew that until recently he could have expected no assistance from the British. But the evangelicals had changed that.

SOURCE 7 A widow committing sati. This picture was painted *c.*1800.

Rammohan Roy became a close friend of Carey, the evangelicals' leader. Together they worked hard to try to end the practice of sati.

In 1829 Roy made a brave decision: he agreed to travel to Britain to try to persuade more British people to support a ban on sati. Some Hindus warned him that travelling overseas would harm his soul forever. Roy dismissed this idea and set sail.

By the end of that year, the British Governor General of India finally decided that the time had come to act. He banned sati throughout British lands in India.

Roy was delighted at this news … but he was *very* unusual. The vast majority of Indians were angry and alarmed. This was a turning point in British rule in India. It was the first time the British had ever used their power to change an Indian custom. Where would it end?

Rammohan Roy died in Bristol in 1833. He is now celebrated in India as a great reformer – but at the time he seemed to have betrayed India by supporting Britain's new desire to interfere with Hindu customs.

ACTIVITY

Make a summary sheet (see page 61) about the story of Rammohan Roy and what it tells us.

◆ The hedge's story

THE GREAT HEDGE OF INDIA

'The story of one of the least-known wonders of Queen Victoria's India . . . Could anything be more astonishing?'
Jan Morris

Roy Moxham

SOURCE 8 Front cover of *The Great Hedge of India* by Roy Moxham.

One day in 1995 a museum worker, Roy Moxham, was browsing through a very old book that he had found in a second-hand shop in London. On one page he read a curious footnote which mentioned that the British had once planted a hedge in India that was almost 2500 kilometres long. He had never heard of this. Other books about India never mentioned it at all. People who knew India well doubted whether this hedge had ever really existed.

But Moxham was hooked: he spent three years following up that one small footnote and wrote a remarkable book (Source 8). The story that he uncovered tells us a lot about how British rule in India was changing by the 1840s.

By 1845 the East India Company controlled huge areas of India. Wherever they went they built roads, bridges and even railways. After banning sati, they also introduced more laws based on Christian standards, and in order to enforce these they had to take charge of law and order and run law courts. All this cost money.

The East India Company made sure that most of the profits from their trade with India went back to Britain. They organised taxes which made it easy for British merchants to sell their goods (such as cotton cloth from the factories of Manchester) in India because Indian businesses could not compete. Britain grew in wealth while huge areas of India remained poor.

The British wanted to raise more money to pay for the cost of governing their land in India – without taking it from their trading profits. They already collected taxes from landowners but they wanted more. They decided to make the most of a way of raising money that rulers in India had used for hundreds of years . . . the salt tax.

Salt is really important in hot climates. Quite apart from making food taste better, it gives essential minerals to the body. Rulers in India knew that they could make money by taxing salt since everyone, rich and poor, needed it. The British, however, raised the salt tax to a far higher level than Indians had ever known before. What is more, the British were determined to make sure that everyone paid the tax. This is where the hedge comes in.

Although the British controlled much of India, there were still many independent 'princely states' which did not follow British rule and had different laws and different taxes (see Source 9). In these areas salt was often far cheaper than it was in British-held lands. Naturally, some Indians realised that they could make a huge profit if they could smuggle cheap salt from these states into British areas and sell it there.

In the 1840s the British planted a hedge where the worst salt smuggling took place. Its tough, sharp thorn bushes could tear the flesh of any smuggler who tried to break through it. It ran for thousands of kilometres and was about four metres high and up to five metres thick. It was like a symbol of the British determination to enforce their laws ... and of the division between the old and new ways of ruling India.

Some historians believe that it was wrong of the British to make the Indians pay far higher taxes than Indian princes ever did. People died because they could not afford the salt. Other historians insist that the British used the money to build roads and canals, and to keep law and order. One way or another, more and more Indians must have resented their British masters in a way that would not have happened if they had just been trading partners.

SOURCE 9 Map of India in 1856, showing the princely states and the Great Hedge.

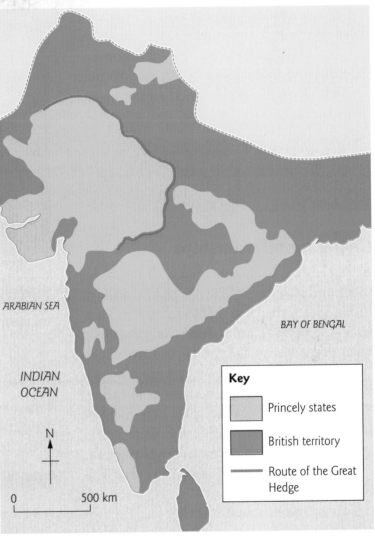

ARABIAN SEA

BAY OF BENGAL

INDIAN OCEAN

N

0   500 km

Key

Princely states

British territory

Route of the Great Hedge

ACTIVITY

Make a summary sheet (see page 61) about the story of the Great Hedge and what it tells us.

◆ *The memsahib's story*

In the early years of the nineteenth century, more and more British women sailed out to India to join their husbands there and raise a family. The Indians called their rulers 'sahibs' and called British wives or daughters 'memsahibs'.

Our next hidden history concerns one of these memsahibs, a young girl we know only as Miss Williams. She grew up in a home very like the one in Source 10, only to meet a shocking death in the blood-stained waters of an Indian river.

DISCUSS A

Compare Source 10 with Source 3 on page 62. How are they different?

Changing relationships

In 1857 Miss Williams lived with her older sister and parents at Cawnpore in northern India. Her father was a colonel in the East India Company's army. Many memsahibs were the wives or daughters of army officers.

Senior officers in the army were always British but most of the soldiers were Indians. They were known as sepoys. There had been a long tradition that the sepoys were proud to serve the British and were loyal to their commanding officers. But by 1857 that was beginning to change.

Part of the problem was that the British officers spent less time with their troops now that their wives were in India. There were other problems too. Sepoy pay had been cut and many sepoys believed that the British were going to force them to drop their Hindu or Muslim beliefs and become Christians. Strains were appearing between the sepoys and their British officers.

In 1857 one Englishman wrote home about how the British were introducing new

SOURCE 10 An engraving of an army officer and his memsahib at breakfast, made in 1842.

laws to change Indian customs and to take land from Indians. He had lived in India for many years and noted that:

SOURCE 11

If a man who left this country thirty years ago were to visit now he would scarcely credit the changes he would see in the treatment of the natives, high and low. The English were not then absolute masters everywhere. Now they are, restraint is cast away ... and they display a supercilious arrogance and contempt of the people.

Of course, a young memsahib like Miss Williams probably knew nothing of these tensions ... until the awful horrors of 1857.

Revolt!

In 1857, some sepoys near Delhi murdered their officers and sparked off a revolt that spread rapidly across the whole of northern India. The violence lasted for almost a year. For a while it seemed that Britain might lose control.

The revolt led to cruelty on both sides. Some of the worst atrocities happened in June 1857 at Cawnpore. Rebels besieged the British army garrison there. Inside were quite a few sepoys who had remained loyal to the British, about 200 British soldiers and many hundreds of women and children. Among these was young Miss Williams.

Day by day, Miss Williams watched as people around her died through wounds, hunger or thirst. Her father was killed early on in the siege. Her mother was shot in the face and took two days to die. Miss Williams was wounded by a bullet in the shoulder but lived to face new horrors.

At the end of June the garrison surrendered. The rebel leader said the British could leave the city by river. But as the unarmed British boarded their boats the fighting broke out once again. The river ran red with blood. Over 250 people were killed. A survivor recorded what happened to Miss Williams:

SOURCE 12

I tell you only what we saw ... children were stabbed and thrown into the river. The schoolgirls were burned to death. I saw their clothes and hair catch fire. In the water a few paces off, by the next boat, we saw the youngest daughter of Colonel Williams. A sepoy was going to kill her with his bayonet. She said, 'My father was always kind to sepoys'. He turned away, and just then a villager struck her on the head with his club and she fell into the water.

Miss Williams died in the river. Perhaps she was lucky. The 200 survivors who were recaptured were later hacked to death by local butchers, despite the attempts of some rebel sepoys to protect them.

DISCUSS B

Can you find any signs from the story of the massacre at Cawnpore that the relationship between the British and the Indians had not completely broken down?

SOURCE 13 A nineteenth-century British painting of the massacre on the river at Cawnpore.

Revenge!

The British called the revolt 'The Indian Mutiny', suggesting that the problems were just within the army. In fact many local princes joined in, especially those who had recently lost land to the British. Maybe they saw this as a chance to get rid of the British for ever. Many Indian historians call the revolt a war of independence. It was certainly long, complicated and violent. As this cartoon from *Punch* (Source 14) shows, the British believed justice was on their side.

SOURCE 14 'Justice', a cartoon from *Punch* magazine, September 1857.

D I S C U S S

How does Source 14 show that the British believed justice was on their side when they crushed the revolt in India?

In fact, British troops often went beyond the search for justice. They wanted revenge. At Cawnpore they arrested anyone they believed to be a rebel and made them lick the floor where the British had been butchered. They tied some rebels to the mouth of a cannon and blew their bodies to pieces. They knew that cows were sacred to Hindus and pigs were unclean to Muslims so they force-fed Hindu rebels with beef and Muslims with pork before hanging them. Others were simply shot by firing squads.

By late 1858 the rebellion was finally over. Law and order had been re-established. But many thousands had died – including young Miss Williams. The British and the Indians had both committed dreadful crimes. Their relationship would never be the same again.

A C T I V I T Y

Make a summary sheet (see page 61) about the story of Miss Williams, the young memsahib, and what it tells us.

◆ *The MP's story*

The mutiny failed but it changed India forever. On 1 November 1858 a proclamation was read out at every railway station in India: the East India Company was abolished and India was to be ruled directly by the British Parliament. All rebels who had not murdered Europeans were pardoned and all Indian religions and ancient customs would be respected. The announcement was followed by a grand firework display.

This was the start of the period known as the 'British Raj'. It lasted from 1858 to 1947. The Indian word 'raj' means 'rule'. Under the British Raj, Queen Victoria was the ruler of all British-held lands in India. (She took the title 'Empress of India' in 1877.) She was represented in India by a viceroy who governed over 300 million Indians, rich and poor, with the help of about 5000 British officials. The army carried on using Indian troops – but it now included far more soldiers from Britain to make sure that there was no repeat of the mutiny.

SOURCE 15 Lord Mayo, the viceroy from 1869 to 1872, summed up the attitude of most British officials in India when he said:

We are all British gentlemen engaged in the magnificent work of governing an inferior [lower] race.

Millions of poor Indians probably did not care what Mayo thought (Source 15), while hundreds of rich princes were just happy that the British Raj allowed them to keep their wealth. Other Indians grew to respect the Raj and its achievements in their country.

However, there were some who were insulted by the attitudes of men like Lord Mayo. Among them was Dadabhai Naoroji (Source 16), another remarkable man whose story is little known in Britain.

Dadabhai was educated at an Indian college run by the British. In 1855 he sailed to England to help run a business there. In London he quickly realised just how little the British people knew about their empire. He decided that it was his duty to educate them. He organised meetings and made speeches about the British Raj. In 1871 Dadabhai made a list of the benefits and failures of British rule in India.

Here are his conclusions:

SOURCE 16 A photograph of Dadabhai Naoroji taken in 1890.

	The benefits of British rule for India:	The failures of British rule:
Humanity	Abolition of sati and of infanticide (the mass killing of unwanted children). Destruction of criminal gangs. Charitable aids in times of famine.	Nothing. Everything is in your favour under this heading.
Civilisation	Education, though yet only partial, is a great blessing. It leads gradually to the destruction of superstition and many evils.	There has been a failure to do as much as could have been done.
Government	Peace and order. Freedom of speech and liberty of the press. Equal justice (but sometimes favouring Europeans). Good service of highly educated administrators.	Repeated breach of pledges to give the natives a fair and reasonable share in running their own country. There is an utter disregard of the feelings and views of the natives.
Wealth	Railways and irrigation. Development of a few valuable products, such as indigo, tea, coffee, silk, etc. Increase of exports. Telegraphs.	Devising new taxes without any effort to improve the people's ability to pay. The great mass of the poor have hardly two pence a day and a few rags. There have been famines that the British could have prevented. There has been a loss of manufacturing industry and skill.

DISCUSS

Look at the table above.

1 What does Naoroji like most about what the British have done in India?
2 What does Naoroji like least about the British in India?
3 How might the British people respond to his views?

Dadabhai did more than just make speeches and write leaflets. Back in India in 1885, he helped to set up the Indian National Congress. This was an organisation that was full of well-educated Indians who were loyal to Queen Victoria. They did not want to end British rule, but they did want responsible Indians – such as themselves – to be given important posts in the government of their own country. The British ignored their demands.

In 1886 Dadabhai returned to England with an extraordinary ambition: he wanted to become a Member of Parliament in Britain. You might imagine that English voters would never choose as an MP someone who dared to criticise the Raj … but you would be wrong. In 1892 Dadabhai won the seat of Central Finsbury in north London by just six votes. He became the first ever Indian Member of Parliament at Westminster.

ACTIVITY

Make a summary sheet (see page 61) of Dadabhai Naoroji's story and what it tells us.

SOURCE 17 This picture shows the House of Commons in 1893. Somewhere amongst all those white, British faces must be the one Indian who had won the right to speak for the millions of people in his country whose lives were ruled by decisions made by this Parliament. Another example of hidden history!

FINAL ACTIVITY

1 Prepare a **large** display graph based on the one shown here. Place each summary sheet where you think it belongs on the graph. You will need to find the right date and then decide how good or bad the relationship between the British and the Indians was at that time.

2 Underneath the graph write a paragraph explaining how the relationship between the Indians and the British changed during this period.

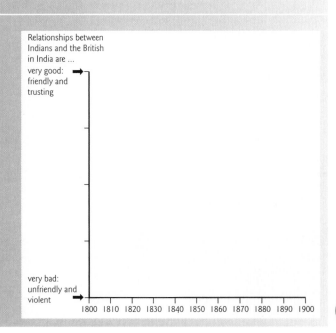

Relationships between Indians and the British in India are …

very good: friendly and trusting

very bad: unfriendly and violent

1800 1810 1820 1830 1840 1850 1860 1870 1880 1890 1900

7 OUT OF AFRICA: WHO SHOULD HAVE THE BENIN HEAD?

Trace the history of the bronze head and decide where it belongs now

If this head could talk it would tell you a very disturbing story
   ... of fear and greed,
   ... of honour and broken promises,
   ... of violence and revenge.
The head would also tell you a lot about one of the most astonishing episodes in the history of the world: the so-called 'Scramble for Africa'.

SOURCE 1 The Benin head, from the Royal Albert Memorial Museum in Exeter.

YOUR ENQUIRY

This bronze head is now in a museum in Exeter. Through this enquiry you will trace the story of the head: where it came from and how it ended up in Exeter. At the end you will decide who should have it now – the people of Britain or the people of Benin, where the head came from originally.

As you make up your mind about the Benin head, you will see how the impact of empire building long ago is still being felt in surprising disputes and arguments facing us today.

◆ *The 'dark continent'*

The story of how the bronze head came from Benin to Exeter begins long ago, in the fifteenth century.

Ships from Europe first sailed down the west coast of Africa in the 1480s. The Europeans set up trading bases and ports. Their ships took on supplies or cargoes of slaves. But these Europeans did not go far inland to explore or to settle. They knew little or nothing about magnificent African kingdoms, such as Benin.

If they had ventured into Africa they would have found:

◆ cities and towns
◆ powerful kings
◆ large empires
◆ trade over long distances
◆ skilful craftspeople – working in bronze, ivory and wood.

The rulers of Benin were called Obas. They were powerful men, in total control of a remarkable kingdom in west Africa.

The people of Benin believed that the Oba was descended from the god who made the world. Only the Oba could carry out important religious rituals, such as the one which ensured that there was a good harvest. In these rituals the Oba was accompanied by elaborately dressed attendants carrying shields and swords.

Craftspeople made fine objects for the Oba to wear in the religious rituals, or at his court. They worked in ivory (from elephant tusks), wood, coral (imported from far away on the other side of Africa), brass and bronze. The bronze heads such as the one shown in Source 1 were made after the death of an Oba. Each one was decorated with ivory, beads, wooden rattles and bells, and put on an altar. It was intended as a permanent and precious reminder of the Oba who had died.

In the years after 1700, the empire of Benin lost much of its land. But its customs, art, religion and the importance of the Obas carried on much as before. These remained unseen and undisturbed by Europeans, who thought of Africa as the 'dark continent'. Then everything changed, in twenty frantic years at the end of the nineteenth century.

DISCUSS

In the 1700s the Europeans called inland Africa the 'dark continent'. What do you think they meant?

◆ *The Scramble for Africa*

By 1880 the British, French and Portuguese had taken over some coastal areas of Africa, but only a few explorers, such as David Livingstone, had travelled far inland. Then, in an extraordinary burst of activity from 1880 to 1900, almost all of Africa was carved up between Europe's leading nations. This has become known as the 'Scramble for Africa'. You can see its effects by comparing Sources 2 and 3.

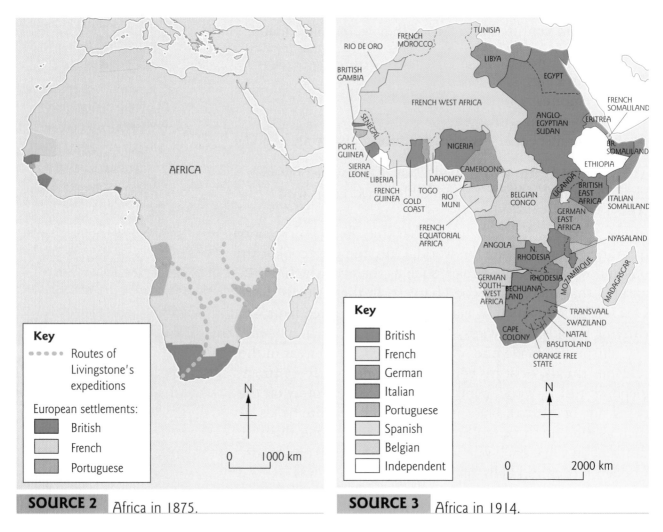

SOURCE 2 Africa in 1875.

SOURCE 3 Africa in 1914.

There is no single reason why European powers started taking African land in such a hurry after 1880. Often they believed it would help their trade. Sometimes they guessed the land might be rich in minerals such as gold or diamonds. Sometimes they hoped that the land would be good for farming.

It reached the point when nations grabbed land just to keep up with others. The King of Belgium took a huge area around the Congo River, saying 'I did not want to miss the chance of getting a piece of this African cake.'

All sorts of people took part in the Scramble for Africa. Match these descriptions to the people in the picture on the right.

◆ **Missionaries** went to spread the Christian faith, to heal the sick and to end certain African customs.
◆ **Explorers** went in search of adventure and new knowledge.
◆ **Traders** went to collect crops and minerals from the heart of Africa – and to find new customers.
◆ **Officials and soldiers** went to protect trade routes so that profits kept flowing.
◆ **Politicians** wanted to please their people by increasing national wealth and pride.

In reality, some people mixed several of these roles: for example, a soldier might have been a keen Christian, or a missionary might also have needed to be an explorer.

SOURCE 4 *An African war scene, 1879.*

No one seemed to consider what the African people thought as their lands were carved up by foreigners. The Europeans drew new boundaries that sometimes split ancient tribal areas. If the Africans tried to fight, European weapons and technology could usually crush their resistance easily (see Source 4).

Over time, Europeans worked hard to improve healthcare and education in many parts of Africa. However, in these early years most Africans were deeply alarmed by the newcomers. One chief, King Mwanga, complained that 'the English have come … they have built a fort, they eat my land, and yet they have given me nothing at all.' He was not the only African leader to suffer at the hands of the English … the Oba of Benin had a similar experience in 1897.

ACTIVITY

Write a short, simple description of what happened between 1880 and 1900 and to explain why you think the events of these years became known as the 'Scramble for Africa'. Try to use words and phrases that capture the idea of a **scramble**!

◆ *The Benin massacre*

Now that you know about the Scramble for Africa, you can make more sense of the next stages in the story of the bronze head of Benin.

ACTIVITY

Choose one of the following characters and as the story is read out listen for what your character does, fails to do, or says. At the end you will think about the ways your character may have helped to cause what eventually happened.

- ◆ The Oba of Benin
- ◆ Captain Gallwey
- ◆ Ralph Moor
- ◆ James Phillips
- ◆ The Oba's generals
- ◆ Ralph Locke
- ◆ Rear Admiral Rawson
- ◆ The politicians in London

SOURCE 5 West Africa and Benin *c.* 1896.

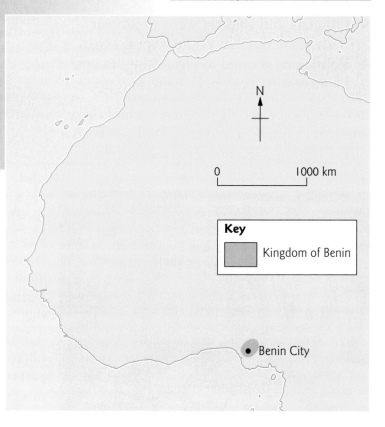

By the 1890s almost all of Africa was controlled by European nations. Along the West African coast, however, one kingdom still insisted on running its own affairs: the kingdom of Benin. In 1892 a British official, Captain Gallwey, travelled from the coast, where most white people were still based, to visit Benin City. He met the Oba (king) of Benin and agreed a treaty. The treaty was written in English and African translators tried to translate the words of the treaty for the Oba, who thought that he was just making a general agreement to trade with the British. In fact the words of the treaty more or less handed control of Benin over to the British.

At first all seemed to go well. The trade in spices and palm oils continued successfully and the British let the Oba rule as he liked. But by 1895 there were problems. The Oba heard how the British had used force to crush nearby African kingdoms and he was angry. He closed the trade routes to the coast. The British official in charge of that area, Ralph Moor, persuaded the Oba to open them again but Moor also sent messages to the politicians in London. He asked them to let him send troops into Benin City, to take full control of the kingdom. The politicians ordered him not to attack because they did not want Britain to be drawn into a war which would be very expensive. Moor must have been angry with this decision: he had used violence to get his way with other African chiefs and believed that it was what they understood best.

A year later Ralph Moor went on leave (holiday) and Captain James Phillips, a newly arrived official, took over. Phillips heard that British traders were angry that profits from Benin had been lower than expected. He wrote to the politicians in London and told them:

SOURCE 6

… I am certain that there is only one remedy: that is to depose the king of Benin. I am convinced that peaceful measures are now quite useless and that the time has come to move the obstruction. I do not expect any serious resistance from the people of the country, but to avoid any danger I wish to take with me sufficient armed force. I would add that I have reason to hope that sufficient riches in ivory may be found in the king's house to pay for the cost of this attack.

Without waiting for a reply to this letter, Phillips sent a message to the Oba telling him that he would be coming to see him in Benin City very soon.

However, the Oba sent messengers back to Phillips to say that he could not receive a visit for at least two months. They explained that the Oba was taking part in a ritual where his body had to be cut and scarred to please the gods and to bring blessings on the land. It would be an insult for foreigners to see him during this time.

Phillips showed no sympathy. He replied telling the Oba that he was far too busy to delay the visit and was coming anyway.

Phillips set off for Benin City early in January 1897. He took with him eight British officials and traders, with their servants. No soldiers accompanied the group.

On the way to Benin City three messengers from the Oba came to meet them. Once again they asked Phillips to turn back or to delay his visit for two days. Phillips refused and his group pushed on towards Benin City. But they never arrived.

On 4 January Phillips and his group reached a narrow forest path. Lying in wait were some of the Oba's generals. They had decided that their master was not being firm enough with the British. Without his knowledge, they had planned to kill Phillips and his party. As the group passed by they leaped upon them with spears and daggers.

Of the nine British men who set out, only two survived and struggled back to the coast. One of them later wrote a book about the ambush and called it *The Benin Massacre*. The name stuck. The other survivor, Ralph Locke, will reappear later in our story.

As soon as news of the ambush in Benin reached London, the politicians decided to punish the Oba. They sent a fleet of ships and marines to Africa under Rear Admiral Rawson, which arrived off the coast of Benin on 4 February. Rawson quickly gathered the various traders of the area, including African chiefs whose people acted as middle-men in the trade between Benin City and the coast. Rawson told the group that 'the Oba was to be no more, his town taken and his priests, if possible, killed, the Juju houses burned and the Benin Juju for ever broken ...'.

'Juju' meant the religion of the people of Benin. The British had always deeply disliked it. To their European minds it was full of susperstition, magic and witchcraft. For years the British had chosen to ignore these beliefs, but now they intended to crush them forever. Perhaps it was the ambush and murder of Captain Phillips that made the British take action. Or it may have been that news was reaching the coast of something even more dreadful that was taking place across Benin: human sacrifice on a massive scale.

In the weeks following the ambush of Captain Phillips, the Oba had guessed that the British would use force to try to end his power. He consulted his SOOTHSAYERS and prayed to the spirits asking how he could save his kingdom. He decided to use human sacrifice. This had been part of Benin's religion for hundreds of years, but in this time of deep crisis the Oba did not just sacrifice one or two humans, but hundreds. When Rawson's troops eventually marched towards Benin City they found hundreds of human corpses at shrines along their path. All this is described in a book written by R.H. Bacon. He called the book *Benin – City of Blood*. More bloodshed was to follow.

Rawson reached Benin City on 18 February 1897. The bows and arrows and the old guns of the Africans were no match for the modern guns, rifles and rocket tubes used by the British. By the end of that same day, Rawson had taken the city. The British set about demolishing or burning outlying huts as they closed in on the royal palace where the Oba lived. Finally the palace and the Oba himself were captured. Within days the palace was burned to the ground. The British claimed that this was an accident but no one can be sure.

The Oba was tried by British law and was banished from Benin for ever. As he was led away to be held captive for the rest of his life, the Oba could see British officers raiding his royal palace. He could only watch as white men carried off the treasures of the Obas of Benin and their mighty empire whose power no one had ever dared challenge. Those days had gone for ever and Benin was now part of a new empire – the British Empire.

Among the British officers claiming treasures from the Oba's palace that day was Ralph Locke, one of the two survivors of the so-called 'Benin massacre'. In his arms he carried a large bronze head. Once this head had been a symbol of the god-given power of the Oba; now it was a sign of the collapse of that power and of the strange period of history that we call the 'Scramble for Africa'.

Ralph Locke took the bronze head back to Britain. Eventually he passed it on to the Royal Albert Museum in Exeter. It now sits in a glass case staring out at visitors who often know little or nothing of how it came to be there and who may pass it by without thinking of what it tells us about the impact of empire.

DISCUSS

1 Which of the characters from the activity on page 78 would you most blame for the destruction of Benin City?
2 Is it fair for us to blame people for things that happened in the past? Explain your reasons.

◆ *So . . . whose head is it?*

The bronze head of Benin has been in the museum in Exeter for over 100 years now. For much of that time Benin remained within the British Empire. It is now part of the republic of Nigeria. There is a new Oba of Benin who is descended from the man who was DEPOSED in 1897. He is one of the rulers of Nigeria. He has been trying to reclaim for the people of Benin the treasures that were taken to Britain in 1897. He has been helped by Bernie Grant, a British Member of Parliament, whose ancestors came originally from Benin. Before Bernie Grant died in 2000 he wrote to every British museum that holds any objects taken from Benin in 1897. He tried to persuade each museum to return the objects to the Oba.

SOURCE 7 Bernie Grant MP.

ACTIVITY

Here are some extracts from Bernie Grant's letter to the museums. They have been mixed up with some extracts from replies he received from the museum curators.

◆ Which statements are Bernie Grant's and how can you tell?
◆ Which statements are the museum curators' and how can you tell?

> The Benin religious and cultural objects were looted in February 1897 from Benin City.

> The objects can also inform UK museum visitors about the history of the British Empire.

> Museums in Nigeria, including the one in Benin itself, already have an excellent range of ivory, carvings and bronze heads.

> Museums have a responsibility to preserve the past so that people can enjoy it and learn from it.

> The destruction of the history of the Benin people was an act of appalling racism, which must be put right. The taking of the objects from Benin is one of the most distasteful and abiding injustices arising out of the European colonisation of Africa.

> The objects introduce millions of UK museum visitors to the remarkable culture and religious beliefs of Benin.

> The British deposed the Oba of Benin in 1897 because he insisted on keeping the independence of his kingdom.

> The British took these objects as part of a battle for trade in Europe's carve up of Africa.

> If the objects are returned to the Oba and not to a Nigerian museum, they may not be seen by the public.

FINAL ACTIVITY

Who should have the head of Benin?

The Royal Albert Museum in Exeter has to decide whether the museum's bronze head should be returned to the Oba in Nigeria. Imagine that it wants to gather the views of people who visit the museum and that it has decided to set up a display or a PowerPoint presentation to explain the issues to the visitors and to seek their views.

Write five sections that will go in the display.

WHO SHOULD HAVE THE HEAD OF BENIN?

◆ In section A – **The background** – explain to the visitors what we mean by the 'Scramble for Africa', e.g. what happened, when it happened and why it happened. Keep it short and accurate and make it interesting (you know how people hate to read long notices in museums!). You could base this on the summary you did on page 77.

◆ In section B – **The head** – tell the story of how Ralph Locke came to own the head. Once again, keep it short, accurate and interesting. You will find what you need on pages 78–81.

◆ In section C – **Keep it?** – make a list of reasons why the museum should KEEP the head. (Include ideas even if you do not agree with them yourself.)

◆ In section D – **Return it?** – make a list of reasons why the museum should RETURN the head to the Oba. (Again, include ideas even if you do not agree with them yourself.) For both C and D you will find reasons on page 82 – but include others that you can think of as well.

◆ In Section E, your final panel or slide should just say **Visitors – what do you think?** Should the museum keep the head or return it, and why?'

Now that you have studied the story behind the Benin head and have prepared your presentation, you should be able to make up your own mind: who do *you* think should have the head of Benin?

8

IMAGES OF EMPIRE: HOW WAS THE BRITISH EMPIRE PORTRAYED?

Tackle the picture challenges to work out what children were expected to think of the British Empire

In 1897 Britain imported more bottles of champagne than ever before. The British people were celebrating Queen Victoria's 60 years on the throne. No British monarch had ever ruled for so long and a new name had to be invented for the celebration – it was called the Diamond Jubilee. At the centre of the festivities was a celebration of the Queen's Empire. During the 60 years of Queen Victoria's reign the British Empire had grown by more than ten times. The Empire now covered nearly a fifth of the Earth's surface and included a quarter of its population. In 1897 the British Empire was simply the largest empire the world had ever known.

On the morning of 22 June 1897 Queen Victoria went to the telegraph room in Buckingham Palace. She pressed an electric button and, within seconds, her Diamond Jubilee message was on its way to the far corners of her empire. The message said simply, 'From my heart I thank my beloved people. May God bless them.'

Later that day the Queen rode in a carriage through the streets of London to St Paul's Cathedral for a service of thanksgiving. The procession included 50,000 British and Empire soldiers from all over the world. Source 1 shows part of the procession with Australia's New South Wales Lancers proudly parading to St Paul's.

SOURCE 1 A photograph of Queen Victoria's Diamond Jubilee procession, 1897.

SOURCE 2 Poster advertising the Jubilee celebrations in Cannington, Somerset.

The Jubilee was also celebrated in towns and villages all over Britain. For several days in June 1897 there were parades, speeches, religious services, balls, street parties and concerts. The poster in Source 2 is advertising the festivities at Cannington in Somerset.

However, not everyone in Britain at the end of the nineteenth century was a strong supporter of the Empire. Some people thought that the whole idea of empire was wrong. Others were ignorant about how the Empire worked. At the turn of the century the imperialists (supporters of empire) thought that it was important to make British citizens, especially children and young people, feel proud of their country and empire. Some of the images you will see in this chapter were designed to do just this. They are therefore useful for finding out what the imperialists wanted the younger generation to think about the Empire.

CANNINGTON.

DIAMOND JUBILEE CELEBRATION

JUNE 22nd, 1897.

A DINNER

Will be given to the WORKING MEN of Cannington, with their WIVES and FAMILIES, above the age of 15 Years, between the hours of 12 and 2, at the "Anchor" Inn.

Application for Dinner Tickets to be made to Mr. Martin not later than June 11th.

A PROCESSION

Will be formed at the "Anchor" headed by the

STOGURSEY BRASS BAND,

AT 2-30 P.M., TO MARCH TO THE PARK.

ATHLETIC SPORTS

Confined to the Parishioners of Cannington,

WILL BE HELD IN THE PARK, and a

TEA FOR THE SCHOOL CHILDREN.

DANCING FROM 7 TO 9.

FIREWORKS AT 9.   BONFIRE AT 10.

N.B.--The Friendly Societies have consented to join the Procession.

GOD SAVE THE QUEEN !!

YOUR ENQUIRY

Queen Victoria's Diamond Jubilee was one way in which British citizens were made to feel proud. But there were many other ways that the British Empire could be promoted. In this enquiry you will find out about the different images of empire which were presented to children and young people. You will have to think hard about the messages behind these images if you want to do well in the picture challenges. Let's begin with the images of the Empire which children would have seen in school.

◆ The Empire in school

The most obvious way to encourage children to value the Empire was through their schools. From 1902 many schools celebrated Empire Day on 24 May each year. The idea was for pupils and teachers to spend a day concentrating on the glories of the British Empire. Pupils learned facts about the Empire and sang PATRIOTIC songs. In some schools children took the parts of heroes from the Empire, such as Robert Clive or James Wolfe. In other schools pupils dressed up to represent people from different colonies, each paying their respects to their 'mother', Britannia (who was often the tallest girl in the school). In these ways schoolchildren created their own images of the British Empire.

SOURCE 3 A photograph of a school's Empire Day celebrations in 1923.

PICTURE CHALLENGE

Look at Source 3.

1 How are the children dressed?
2 What are the children doing?
3 What messages about the British Empire were reinforced on Empire Day?

Not everyone in Britain agreed with Empire Day. Some people thought that children were being brainwashed into supporting the British Empire. However, most schools joined in, perhaps because the afternoon was a holiday!

Schoolchildren also learned about the Empire from maps in their textbooks and on their classroom wall. This map of the world was made in 1886. Britain's territories are coloured pink. The map exaggerates the size of Britain compared to other countries. If you look carefully at the map you will also find lots of other messages about the British Empire.

SOURCE 4   A map of the British Empire in 1886.

PICTURE CHALLENGE 2

Look at Source 4.

1 Find out the meanings of the words at the top of the map. What do these words tell us about British attitudes towards the Empire?
2 At the sides and bottom of the map are people and symbols from Britain's colonies. Identify as many of these as you can. What do the symbols suggest about British attitudes towards the colonies?
3 How does the map show that Britain gained her empire through navy and sea power?
4 Write a short paragraph to sum up the message behind the map.

◆ *The Empire in fiction*

A hundred years ago children and young people did not watch television, surf the internet or play computer games; they read magazines, comics and novels. Many of these publications featured stories set overseas in the British colonies. Children loved these exciting adventures that took place in strange lands. However, many of the stories portrayed the British as heroes, while the native people appeared as either servants or savages. You can see some of these images in Sources 5–7.

SOURCE 6 The front cover of a boys' magazine from 1924.

SOURCE 5 The front cover of a children's storybook from 1926.

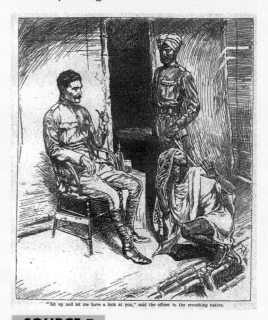

SOURCE 7 An illustration from a story in a magazine, 1917.

PICTURE CHALLENGE 3

Look at Sources 5–7.

1 How did these images try to glorify Britain, or British people?
2 How did these images suggest that the native people were inferior to the British?
3 Which of these images would be considered most offensive today?

◆ *The Empire in advertising*

Another way in which children were shown images of the Empire was in advertisements. At the beginning of the twentieth century many companies used the Empire to boost sales of their products. The examples in Sources 8–10 show some of the ways the Empire was used in advertising.

SOURCE 8

SOURCE 9

SOURCE 10

PICTURE CHALLENGE 4

For each advertisement in Sources 8–10:

1 work out what product was being advertised
2 describe the images of empire contained in the advertisement
3 explain why you think the advertisers used these images of empire.

◆ *The Empire and Scouting*

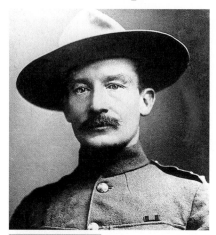

SOURCE 11 A photograph of Lieutenant General Robert Baden-Powell, 1907.

Look at Source 11. In 1907 this man founded the Boy Scout movement. He is Lieutenant General Robert Baden-Powell. Baden-Powell was a soldier in the British army who became a national hero during Britain's war against the Boers in South Africa. He wanted Britain's boys to grow up into strong and active citizens who would be able to defend the British Empire. Scouts had to follow the Scout Law at all times. This meant that they had to be:

◆ trustworthy
◆ loyal to their king and country
◆ helpful to others
◆ obedient to their parents or Scout leader
◆ cheerful at all times!

In the years after 1907 tens of thousands of boys joined the Scouts. In 1910 the Girl Guide movement was formed in order to give girls similar experiences. Scouting soon spread across the British Empire.

SOURCE 12 A photograph showing Robert Baden-Powell with Scouts from different parts of the Empire at the Imperial Jamboree, London, 1924.

Robert Baden-Powell's book, *Scouting for Boys*, became a huge best-seller after its publication in 1908. The book contained details of the Scout Law as well as practical advice and stories of adventure at home and abroad.

SOURCE 13 A Scouting Association publicity photograph, 1910.

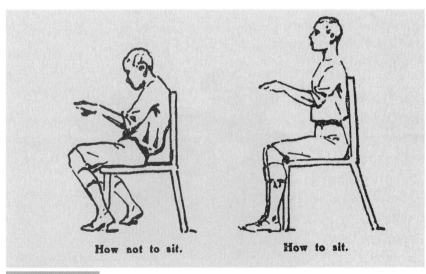

How not to sit.   How to sit.

SOURCE 14 An illustration from *Scouting for Boys*, 1908.

PICTURE CHALLENGE 5

Source 12
1 Do you think this picture was an official or an unofficial photograph?
2 What is the message of the photograph?

Source 13
3 Why do you think this picture might persuade boys to join the Scouts?

Source 14
4 What does this picture tell us about Baden-Powell's attitudes?

◆ *Lantern slides of the Empire*

At the end of the nineteenth century lantern slide shows were a popular form of entertainment. During the winter months, adults and children would crowd into village halls, schools, theatres and church rooms to see photographs or pictures projected onto large screens. In 1907 the Colonial Office in London came up with a special scheme to teach children about the British Empire. They planned a series of lantern slide shows about life in different parts of the Empire. Once again, the aim was to make children feel proud to be citizens of the British Empire.

The Colonial Office appointed an official photographer, Hugh Fisher. Fisher was paid to travel around the British Empire for three years, taking thousands of photographs for the lantern slide shows. Before Fisher left Britain in October 1907, the Colonial Office instructed him to take photographs of . . .

... the native characteristics of the country and the super-added characteristics due to British rule.

DISCUSS

1 What do you think the Colonial Office's instruction meant?
2 Why do you think the Colonial Office gave this instruction?

Hugh Fisher first travelled to India. He sent back hundreds of pictures and the Colonial Office selected the ones which would be used. On the following pages you will find a small sample of Fisher's photographs. Of course, the photographs give us a very selective and one-sided view of British India. They represent the official, Colonial Office, view. However, they are very useful for finding out the way in which the Empire was portrayed to British children.

SOURCE 15 St Mary's Church in Madras.

SOURCE 16 A Fakir (Hindu holy man) sitting on

SOURCE 17 Snake charmers at Benares.

SOURCE 18 A view of the Lansdowne Bridge over the river Indus.

SOURCE 19 A burning ghat (cremation) at Benares.

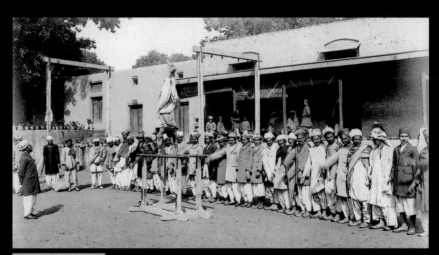

SOURCE 20 A gymnastics class at the Government High School, Peshwar.

YOUR FINAL PICTURE CHALLENGE

Imagine that you are an official at the Colonial Office in 1907. You can select three of Hugh Fisher's photographs to include in one of the lantern slide shows about British India.

Look again at the instructions that the Colonial Office gave to Fisher (page 92). Now select your three photographs from pages 93–95. Write a short report explaining what message you hope each of the photographs will convey about British India.

9

END OF EMPIRE: WHAT PERSUADED THE BRITISH TO QUIT INDIA IN 1947?

Write a letter to Lord Mountbatten persuading him to grant India independence

These two men look worlds apart don't they? Yet in 1947 they were drawn together to try to tackle an enormous problem: they had to decide when and how the British should finally leave India.

On the left is Lord Louis Mountbatten, the viceroy of India. He was in India to represent King George VI, emperor of India, making decisions that affected the lives of the millions of Indians living under British rule.

On the right is Mohandas Gandhi. Over the previous fifty years, Gandhi had become a representative of millions of Indians as he struggled to persuade the British that the people of India should be allowed to rule themselves. Gandhi had recently run a campaign that called upon the British to 'Quit India'. But they were still there . . .

YOUR ENQUIRY

In this chapter you will imagine that it is February 1947. You must write a letter to Lord Mountbatten as if you are a supporter of Gandhi. You are determined that the British must leave India very soon. In your letter you will use your knowledge of India's history to persuade Mountbatten that the time has come for the British to 'Quit India'.

◆ *Promises, promises . . .*

The British had always publicly stated that they were not ruling India for their own benefit. As you saw in Chapter 2, the British first went to India to trade and only later took control of more and more of the land. As they became more deeply involved in ruling India, they made bold statements to show that they remained there only in order to improve it.

In 1858, following the Indian uprising of 1857 (described in Chapter 6), control of India was taken out of the hands of the East India Company. Parliament passed the Government of India Act which set up the British Raj (raj is the Indian word for rule), under a viceroy as a sort of deputy-king.

SOURCE 1 The Act stated that the British Parliament and the viceroy would:

. . . rule India for the benefit of all our subjects there.

SOURCE 2 In 1900 the viceroy of India was Lord Curzon. Here is what he said about the reason why Britain still held power over India:

If I felt that we were not working here for the good of India . . . then I would see the link that holds England and India together broken without a sigh. But it is because I believe in the future of this country and in the capacity of our own race to guide it to goals that it has never before attained, that I keep courage and press forward.

ACTIVITY

Begin your letter to Lord Mountbatten. He is an important man and you will need to choose your words carefully or he may ignore what you say. In your introduction you should remind him that in 1858 Britain promised to rule India in order to help its people. You could begin like this . . .

February 1947

To His Excellency Lord Mountbatten, viceroy of India

Sir,

I congratulate you on your recent appointment as His Majesty's viceroy in India. I am writing to persuade you to use your power to end the British Raj as soon as you possibly can.

I will give you many reasons why the British should leave India, but first I must remind you that your people have always claimed that they took control of our land in order to help us. For example . . .

(Now use some words from the sources above and explain how they show that this **is** what the British have said.)

◆ *The day of shame at Amritsar*

You have already looked at the table on page 72, in which Dadabhai Naoroji listed the good and bad things about British rule as he saw it. Most historians would agree that Britain can take some credit for much of its work in India. But on 13 April 1919 there occurred the most shameful day in the history of the Raj. Here is what happened.

After the First World War (1914–18) India was very unsettled. Many Indians felt that the time had come to run their own affairs as an independent country. Angry crowds gathered all over India.

The British are happy for thousands of Indians to die in the war fighting for the Empire . . .

. . . but they still won't let us run our own land.

The politicians in Europe are creating new nations like Poland that are allowed to rule themselves . . .

. . . but they won't let it happen here.

In Russia the people have taken power by a violent revolution . . .

. . . maybe we could do the same?

The British feared that the Indians might turn to terrorism and violence so they passed the Rowlatt Act. The Act allowed the British to imprison anyone they thought was a political trouble-maker. This just made matters worse.

The Indian people were furious. Millions took to the streets. Some demonstrated peacefully, but others did not. In the north-western city of Amritsar, mobs ran out of control, storming two banks, stealing cash and murdering then burning three white staff. An English missionary was pulled from her bicycle and brutally assaulted.

The British were determined to restore order. On 12 April 1919 they banned all processions and public meetings in Amritsar. It did no good. The next day thousands of unarmed Indians defied this order and crowded into a large enclosed area of wasteland known as the Jallianwala Bagh. A speaker climbed onto a pile of rubble and began to read a poem of liberty. The scene was now set for the most terrible event in the history of the British Raj.

As the meeting began, there was a sound of rumbling engines and marching feet. Reginald Dyer, the soldier in charge of the British forces in Amritsar, had brought two armoured cars and about one hundred troops to teach the Indians a lesson.

Dyer ordered his soldiers to line up facing the crowd. He gave no final warning. He gave the order to fire.

The troops began shooting directly into the crowd and continued non-stop for ten minutes. The protesters panicked. They rushed towards the two exits but the gunfire cut them down. As bodies fell, people stumbled and were trampled in the crush. Some were shot as they tried to climb the high walls surrounding the Jallianwala Bagh, others threw themselves down a deep well in a desperate attempt to escape.

When it was all over, Dyer made no attempt to help the wounded. Night fell soon afterwards and no Indians were allowed on the streets after dark. The bodies lay there as wild animals came to eat their fill.

Months later, the British held an enquiry into Dyer's actions. The report established that 1600 bullets had been fired and 379 people had been killed. Dyer was forced to resign. His actions kept Amritsar under control for the short term, but, to this day, the Amritsar massacre is remembered in India as the day when the British lost their right to rule.

ACTIVITY

It is time to write the next paragraph of your letter to Lord Mountbatten. Remember that you are trying to persuade him to end British rule. Do not just write down the whole story of the Amritsar massacre. Pick out the best points to make him feel that the British lost the right to rule India by their actions at Amritsar.

You could try to answer in advance some points that Mountbatten might make about Amritsar, for example he might say:

'What happened was tragic – but we had to restore law and order.'
'It never happened again. This was not the way we usually kept order.'

◆ *The Great Soul*

Pressure on the British to give more power to the Indian people came from the Congress Party. This party had been founded in 1885 by educated Indians like Dadabhai Naoroji, who you read about in Chapter 6. The Party admired the British and it tried to achieve its aims by quiet discussion. Gandhi, a successful lawyer, joined the Congress Party but soon began to change its approach. His friend Jawaharlal Nehru led the party while Gandhi developed his own methods to show the British that they were in the wrong and that they must grant India independence.

Gandhi was deeply impressed by Hindu holy writings in the *Baghavad Gita*. He also admired the prophet Mohammed and this command of Jesus Christ: '*Do not resist one who is evil. But if anyone strikes you on the right cheek, turn to him the other cheek as well.*' He took these words seriously and believed that the person who never used violence was stronger than the one who did.

Gandhi turned these ideas into a non-violent way of resisting injustice. He called his method *satyagraha*, which means 'truth force'. Gandhi taught people who wanted to use satyagraha that they must accept these principles:

- *Your action must have a clear and limited aim (e.g. to end an unfair law).*
- *Before you take any action you must tell your opponents exactly what you are going to do.*
- *You must never humiliate your opponents. Your action should enlighten their minds so that they willingly do what you want.*
- *You should accept a less than perfect solution if necessary.*
- *You must never use violence, even in self defence.*
- *You must be willing to suffer and die for the cause.*

In the 1920s, Gandhi and his followers (including Nehru) applied these principles as they led many peaceful strikes, demonstrations and protests against British rule.

The British often put them in prison, but as soon as they were released they began another non-violent action. It was patience like this that made an Indian poet give Gandhi the title Mahatma, which means 'Great Soul'. But Gandhi was not just a saintly man – he was crafty as well, as he showed in his famous Salt March.

SOURCE 3 Part of a letter from Gandhi to the viceroy before his Salt March in 1930.

My ambition is no less than to convert the British people through non-violence, and to make them see the wrong they have done India. I do not seek to harm your people. I want to serve them as I serve my own.

The Salt March

You found out in Chapter 6, in the story of the Great Hedge, that the British government controlled the making and selling of salt in India – and it took half the price in tax. This was widely resented as it affected every single person. Gandhi decided to protest against the tax. He knew this would attract the support of the poorest villagers and it would show the world how unfair the British were to their Indian subjects. It would also show the British that they could not rule India without the agreement of its people.

Gandhi told the British government that he was going to walk 400 kilometres from his home village to the sea where he would break the law by making salt. He set off on 12 March 1930 and by the time he reached the sea thousands were following him. They watched as the 'Great Soul' made salt and as he quietly defied the British to arrest him once again. Gandhi made sure that there were reporters and film crews from all over the world in the crowds.

SOURCE 4   A photograph of Gandhi on the Salt March.

The British arrested Gandhi for making salt illegally, but within a few days Indians everywhere were defying the law and making their own salt. There were no massacres this time. Some rioting did break out but processions were usually non-violent as Gandhi's trained supporters acted as voluntary police. However, some protesters were killed by guards who beat them to death as they peacefully tried to occupy a salt factory.

All over the world people began to put pressure on the British government to give in. The viceroy had to make a compromise with Gandhi. He released him from prison and invited him to his palace for talks. The Raj was no longer issuing orders, it was joining in discussions.

The viceroy did not grant India independence straight away, but Gandhi did not expect that. By talking with the viceroy and with politicians in London, he helped to persuade the British to allow Indians to vote for their own Parliament of Indian politicians. The Congress Party won the elections that were held in 1937 and was soon running many – but not all – aspects of Indian life. They must have believed that complete independence was just around the corner. But the outbreak of the Second World War in 1939 changed all that.

A CTIVITY

Now write the third paragraph of your letter to persuade Lord Mountbatten that he must give India its complete independence.

◆ Remind Mountbatten how Gandhi used non-violent methods to show that the British could not rule without the agreement of the Indian people.

◆ Tell him how and why an earlier viceroy came to see that the Indians deserved more control over their lives.

◆ You could use some *rhetorical* questions, for example 'Did Gandhi's famous Salt March teach you nothing?' or 'Can't you see that we are stronger than you?'

'Give us chaos!'

As soon as the Second World War started in September 1939, the viceroy announced that Indians would fight for the British Empire all over the world. Nehru was furious (see Source 5), but many Indians did fight loyally and thousands died during the war.

The British promised to grant independence to India as soon as possible after the war ended. The viceroy told Gandhi that it would create chaos if the British left too soon. Gandhi replied 'Then give us chaos!' He simply wanted Indians to be allowed to run their own affairs straight away.

SOURCE 6 A photograph of Indian soldiers serving in Italy in 1944.

SOURCE 5 Nehru said of the decision to send Indians to fight in the Second World War:

There is something rotten when one man, and a foreigner and representative of a hated system, can plunge 400 million human beings into war without a slightest reference to them.

In 1942 Gandhi began the Quit India campaign of non-violent protest, but it was increasingly difficult to control the protests and there was serious rioting.

Another problem rose to the surface during the war: the age-old tension beween Hindus and Muslims. The Muslims were heavily outnumbered by Hindus and feared that they would be treated as second-class citizens once the British left. Their leader, Mohammad Ali Jinnah, (see Source 7), insisted that the Muslims should be given a country of their own when independence was finally granted. He wanted India to be 'partitioned'. The longer the British stayed, the deeper they would be drawn into the conflict between Hindus and Muslims.

SOURCE 7
Mohammad Ali Jinnah.

Shortly after the war ended in 1945 Britain's new Prime Minister, Clement Attlee, promised to grant independence to India very soon. Perhaps he had been persuaded by Gandhi's non-violent protest, or perhaps he just thought India was uncontrollable. Or maybe he had noticed that Britain was no longer making anything like as much money from its trade with India as it once had.

Whatever the reason, Attlee announced that the British would leave India in June 1948 at the latest. In February 1947 he sent a new viceroy, Lord Louis Mountbatten, to organise the last days of the British Empire in India. For some Indians it could not come quickly enough!

ACTIVITY A

It is now time to write the final part of your letter to Lord Mountbatten.

Use the information on this page to persuade him that the British should leave India even earlier than June 1948. You should find plenty of reasons to give him, but be sure to use them persuasively. He won't be impressed by just a list.

◆ *Partition*

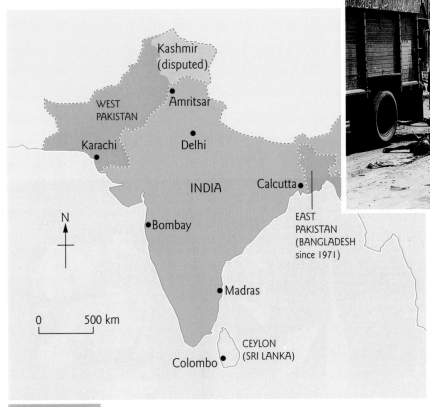

SOURCE 8 India and Pakistan, August 1947.

SOURCE 9 A photograph of victims of riots being cleared from the streets, 1947.

The story of the 'end of empire' in India has a terrible and tragic ending.

Lord Mountbatten eventually gave India her independence even earlier than Attlee had promised. The British Raj ended on 15 August 1947. But India did not remain as one single nation. Jinnah got his way and the Muslims won their own nation, called Pakistan. It occupied the two main areas of Muslim population, in north-west and north-east India.

In the months before the partition there was terrible violence between Muslims and Hindus, but even worse was to follow after partition. More than 10 million Hindus had to leave their homes and move to the right side of the new frontiers. As they flooded across the country, through towns and cities where they were not welcome, there was bloodshed on a massive scale. Muslims killed Hindus and Hindus killed Muslims.

Trainloads of people were massacred, roaming gangs attacked and murdered those who travelled on foot. At Amritsar, where the deaths of 379 people in 1919 had caused such shame, thousands now died in the streets, killed by their fellow Indians.

Gandhi did all he could to persuade Hindus to stop attacking Muslims – but this was to cost him his life. In 1948 a Hindu extremist who hated the way Gandhi had defended Muslims shot the Great Soul in cold blood. India had won her independence but she had paid a terrible price.

ACTIVITY B

Look back over your letter to Lord Mountbatten. Do you want to change it in the light of what actually happened? Did Mountbatten and Attlee get the British out of India TOO fast?

10

THE GOOD, THE BAD AND THE UGLY: WHY DO PEOPLE DISAGREE ABOUT THE IMPACT OF EMPIRE?

Write an essay to show that you understand interpretations of history

SOURCE 1 A photograph of Jomo Kenyatta being sworn in as the new Prime Minister of Kenya, 1963.

On 12 December 1963 the people of Kenya celebrated the end of British rule. This photograph shows the ceremony at which Jomo Kenyatta became the Prime Minister of an independent Kenya. Ten years before, a British judge had sentenced Kenyatta to seven years in prison for resisting British rule in Kenya. Now the British smiled and wished the new nation well as they handed over power to him as Prime Minister.

After the Second World War, Britain's grip on its empire began to slip. Britain lacked the money and military strength to maintain such a huge empire. America was now the world's leading nation and Britain was losing its power. Attitudes were also changing. People were determined to create a fairer society. In 1948 Britain and other countries signed the Universal Declaration of Human Rights, which began 'All human beings are born free and equal in dignity and in rights ...'.

The idea of a small country like Britain ruling a huge empire seemed out of step with the modern world. In the years after 1945 most of Britain's colonies gained their independence. The Empire became the COMMONWEALTH – an organisation of independent, free countries.

The map below shows how Britain's colonies gradually gained independence in the period between the end of the Second World War and the early 1980s.

DISCUSS

1 Which countries gained independence during the first wave of decolonisation in the late 1940s?
2 Which countries became independent in the next wave of decolonisation, during the late 1950s and early 1960s?

SOURCE 2

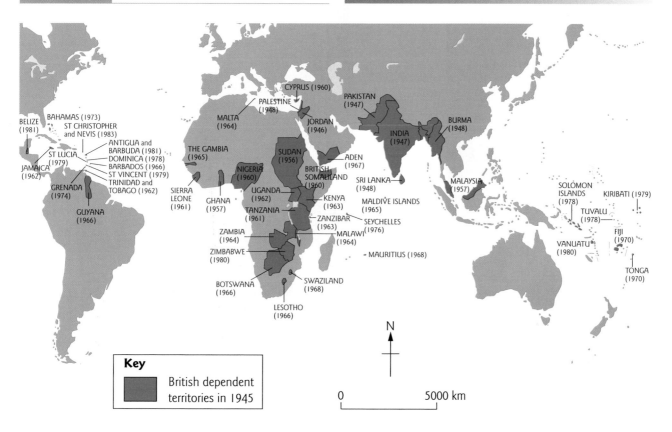

Key

British dependent territories in 1945

N

0   5000 km

YOUR ENQUIRY

We have seen that the British Empire came to a sudden end in the years after the Second World War. In this final enquiry you will find out why people disagree about the impact of empire. Many people argue that it is totally wrong for one group of people to dominate another. In other words, imperialism was wicked and that is the end of the matter. Others argue that the British Empire brought benefits to many people and that it had a positive impact on the world.

It is time to find out why people have such different views.

◆ *Two historians disagree*

Denis Judd and Lawrence James are two respected historians who have both written important books about the British Empire. When Judd and James were asked whether the British Empire was a bad thing they made very different judgements.

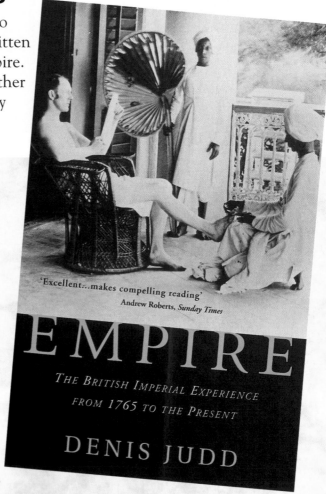

'Excellent...makes compelling reading'
Andrew Roberts, *Sunday Times*

EMPIRE

THE BRITISH IMPERIAL EXPERIENCE FROM 1765 TO THE PRESENT

DENIS JUDD

SOURCE 3 Denis Judd and the front cover of his book, *Empire*.

SOURCE 4 Denis Judd:

The British Empire was a force for bad in the world. *When imperialists boasted that 'the sun never set on the British Empire', critics said that this was because God didn't trust the British in the dark. Much of what the British got up to in their empire was selfish and destructive.*

Imperialists pretended that imperial rule was based on the consent of the colonised people, but the British Empire could never be based on consent. Colonised people were given no say in the running of the colonies. Territories were annexed to serve British needs, not to improve the lives of colonised people. The British often created divisions between people in their colonies. It is not surprising that in many colonies tribal and ethnic conflict followed independence.

Imperial rule damaged the economies of different colonies. Before colonisation many territories were self-sufficient in food. Under British rule colonies were often dependent on one cash crop such as rubber, sugar or coffee. After independence a sharp fall in the price for one of these crops could result in poverty and hunger for millions of people.

Perhaps the worst damage was to the self-esteem of colonised people. The British treated the people they ruled like children. To be ruled by people from a distant land who often tried to destroy aspects of your culture was a humiliating experience.

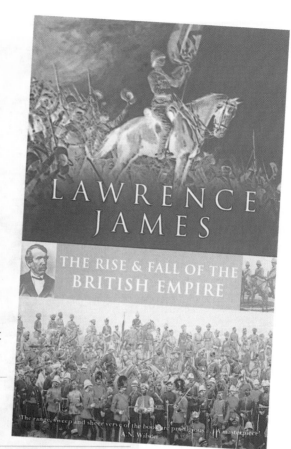

SOURCE 5 Lawrence James and the front cover of his book, *The Rise and Fall of the British Empire*.

SOURCE 6 Lawrence James:

The British Empire was a force for good in the world.

At first the Empire was about making money, but during the nineteenth and twentieth centuries the British Empire improved the lives of millions of people.

The Empire was governed for the benefit of its subjects. The Empire was never perfect, but colonial rulers were honest and dedicated men who were often respected by colonised people. The British Empire was run according to the rule of law. Colonial officials could not do as they wished, but had to answer to Parliament in London.

The British Empire took science and technology to many different parts of the world. British-built railways, bridges and canals improved communications in many territories. Hospitals and medical centres led to better health care.

Important cultural changes took place in British colonies. Colonised people were educated in British schools and attended Christian churches. English was widely spoken throughout the Empire and this means that former British colonies are in a strong position to trade and prosper in the modern world.

It is a great tribute to the British Empire that when it was dismantled after the Second World War there was very little bloodshed.

ACTIVITY

1 Write a list of the arguments that Judd and James make about the impact of the British Empire.

2 How do Judd and James disagree about:

◆ the economic impact of the British Empire
◆ the cultural impact of the British Empire
◆ the way the British Empire was ruled?

◆ *Did the British Empire improve people's lives?*

Health and disease

The colonists carried diseases overseas which killed millions of non-Europeans who had no immunity to European diseases. In North America, Australia and New Zealand colonisation resulted in a huge decline in the native populations. In India and Africa colonial rule resulted in an increase in diseases already established there. This was because the Empire led to more mobility of people, which meant the spread of infection.

Most of the early attempts to improve health in the colonies were aimed at keeping Europeans alive. However, by the end of the nineteenth century mission hospitals and dispensaries in the colonies also provided medical care for Africans and Indians.

SOURCE 7 A photograph showing a mission hospital in Burma, 1891.

This photograph was supplied by the Leprosy Mission, www.leprosymission.org.

But death rates only started to fall in India in the 1920s and even later in Africa.

Communications

The British Empire made huge improvements to communications in many parts of the world. Before colonisation goods were carried by human porters, pack animals and carts. From the middle of the nineteenth century steam railways were built in many British colonies. Railways made it possible to carry huge quantities of goods quite cheaply. The Canadian prairies could now produce grain which could be easily distributed, and the factories of Bombay and Calcutta could be supplied with cotton.

The money and technology for railways came from Britain and it was always the British who decided what sort of railway system should be built. Railways were planned mainly to take cheap raw materials to the ports and to move troops around the colony. They were not built to help colonised people to visit their relatives or take their goods to market.

Agriculture

The Empire provided food and raw materials for Britain. As part of the British Empire, the colonies had a ready-made market for their goods. In many tropical colonies, the British encouraged peasants to grow cash crops such as coffee, palm oil or sugar instead of the foods that they needed to survive. When the price of a cash crop fell, colonised people could face real poverty and hunger.

In many parts of the Empire, the British organised agriculture into plantations. These were large farms which produced one crop. This was often a more efficient way to produce food and raw materials. But many colonisers used a system known as indentured labour on the plantations. Men and women from India or the Pacific Islands agreed to work for five years on a plantation in another part of the Empire. The low wages and brutality of indentured labour gave plantations a bad image.

Industry

In some colonies such as Canada and Australia white settlers began to build factories in the second half of the nineteenth century. But in colonies where the British government had more control it did not usually encourage industry. Before the 1950s there was very little modern industry in any of Britain's African colonies apart from Southern Rhodesia. Some people think that this was a deliberate plan: that the British were afraid that new factories in the colonies would be able to produce goods at a cheaper price, which might put British firms out of business.

> The real reason for the lack of industry was that demand for manufactured goods in the colonies was too limited. Colonised people simply did not have the money to buy factory-produced goods. There was no deliberate plan to hold back industry in the colonies.

ACTIVITY

Much of the information on these pages can be used to support Denis Judd's view that the British Empire had a negative impact on colonised people. But some of the information can be used to support Lawrence James' view that the Empire had a positive impact.

Copy this chart and use the information in this section to collect as many points as you can to support each interpretation.

	Points which support Judd	Points which support James
Health & disease		
Communications		
Agriculture		
Industry		

◆ *Was the spread of British culture a good thing?*

Missionaries

SOURCE 8 A missionary in Africa, 1880.

From the end of the eighteenth century people known as missionaries worked throughout the British Empire. The missionaries saw it as their duty to convert people to Christianity. Many of them thought that most non-European religions and cultures were worthless. The missionaries thought that it was their duty to persuade colonised people to leave their old beliefs and to worship the Christian God.

In nearly all British territories huge numbers of people flocked to the mission stations built by the missionaries. There they were sometimes given food and medical treatment as well as the Bible. For many people Christianity provided answers to questions about evil in the forms of poverty, disease or other misfortunes. It also offered the hope of spending the afterlife in heaven. Millions of people throughout the Empire converted to Christianity.

Schools

This photograph was taken in 1902. It shows a group of Australian Aborigine children at a school run by the British.

DISCUSS

What does Source 9 tell us about education in this part of the Empire?

SOURCE 9 A photograph showing a school for Aborigine children in Australia.

Schools like the one in Source 9 could be found in many parts of the Empire during the nineteenth and twentieth centuries. Often they were attached to mission stations. The schools were used to spread knowledge and British culture around the world. Many colonised people wanted their children to attend school. They saw education as the key to a good job and a better standard of living. In many colonies the schools produced an educated elite of native people.

> Only a tiny minority of children were educated. In 1921 the Gold Coast in Africa had over 200 schools, but these could only provide education for four per cent of children.

The English language

One of the most important effects of the British Empire was the spread of the English language. Today, English has become the main form of communication in the world. This has brought huge advantages to countries that were once British colonies.

In Canada, Australia and New Zealand the large numbers of white settlers meant the inevitable spread of the English language. But this also meant that the culture and language of Native Americans, Aborigines and Maoris were wrecked. In Africa and Asia fewer white people settled. Instead, the British tried to promote the use of English among native people. They believed that it would make ruling easier and would enable people from different regions to communicate with each other.

However, in Africa and Asia it was only the educated few who spoke and wrote English. Most people were simply too poor to learn. Even educated people sometimes felt that being forced to learn another language in order to make a success of your life was wrong. This is what Gandhi had to say:

> ... to give millions of people a knowledge of English is to enslave them. Is it not a painful thing that if I want to go to a court of justice I must use the English language?

ACTIVITY

Make another chart like the one in the activity on page 109. This time use these headings:

	Points which support Judd	Points which support James
Missionaries		
Schools		
English language		

◆ *Was the British Empire brutal?*

European colonisation lasted for nearly 500 years. In that time the Europeans conquered and controlled much of the world. In many territories European settlers took over the best land, forcing native people into poorer areas. Colonialism created vast wealth, but most of this came to Europe. The colonial era set up an unfair pattern of world trade which is still with us today.

In some cases white soldiers and settlers brutally destroyed cultures which had existed for thousands of years. Aztecs, Incas, North American Indians, Maoris and Aborigines were all defeated by European guns. One of the most brutal aspects of empire was the slave trade. For over 200 years Britain and other European countries forced millions of Africans into slavery, as you read in Chapter 4.

The British Empire, like other European empires, was based on racism. Europeans thought that they were superior to other races and could therefore hold power over them. It is no wonder that the leaders of independence movements, like Gandhi, felt that British rule was unfair and should be ended:

> Why do I regard the British rule as a curse? It has impoverished the people of India by a system of exploitation. It has reduced us politically to SERFDOM. It has sapped the foundations of our culture.

British rule resulted in the exploitation of millions of people, but it is more difficult to decide whether it was brutal. It is hard to decide because:

◆ the British Empire was vast and it is hard to make generalisations about how the British treated colonised people

◆ the attitudes and behaviour of British rulers changed during the period of colonial rule
◆ British people at home and in the colonies had different views about how to treat colonised people.

Even when we study just one example of brutality, it is possible to reach different conclusions …

The Morant Bay rebellion, 1865

In the 1860s the island colony of Jamaica was an unhappy place. Many of the old sugar plantations were in ruin. It was more than 30 years since the British had abolished slavery in the Empire. The African Caribbeans of Jamaica were free, but many were without jobs and lived in poverty. The white plantation owners who remained lived in fear that the ex-slaves would start a rebellion. They began to take a harsher attitude towards the black population and they were supported by the governor of the island, Edward John Eyre.

SOURCE 10 Paul Bogle.

The man in Source 10 is Paul Bogle. In October 1865, Paul Bogle led 400 African Caribbeans in an attack on the court house at Morant Bay. Bogle and his men were protesting against the recent harsh sentences which the white magistrates had imposed. The rebels set fire to the court house and killed the magistrates. Some were chopped to pieces; others were beaten to death with clubs; one had his throat cut. The rebels killed seventeen white people and one black man who they said 'had a black skin and a white heart'.

Edward John Eyre, the governor of Jamaica, took immediate action. What followed was one of the most brutal and shameful episodes in the history of the British Empire. Eyre ordered his troops to stop the rebellion. Hundreds of soldiers searched the Jamaican hills for the rebels. When they came to an African–Caribbean village they burnt it.

In the five weeks following the rebellion, 439 black people were shot or hanged and at least 600 were brutally flogged. One woman was flogged to make her reveal where Paul Bogle was hiding: she got 25 lashes first, another 25 a quarter of an hour later, another 25 half an hour later still and was then left all night with a rope around her neck as a warning of what was to come.

When news of Eyre's actions reached England there was uproar. One newspaper headline read, 'TWELVE MILES OF DEAD BODIES'. The British government sent a Commission of Inquiry to Jamaica. The Commission criticised Governor Eyre for his brutality and he was removed from his post, but some important people in Britain thought that Eyre should be punished further. Others supported what Eyre had done. The arguments raged for two years. Three times the case went to the courts, but Eyre was cleared each time.

DISCUSS

1 What made the Morant Bay rebellion such a brutal event?
2 How does the reaction in Britain to the rebellion show that people were shocked by the brutality?

FINAL ACTIVITY

It is time to write an essay explaining why people have such different views about the impact of empire. You can use the paragraph openers below to help you.

Historians such as Lawrence James and Denis Judd have very different views about the impact of the British Empire …

It is not easy to decide whether the British Empire improved people's lives …

People also disagree about whether the spread of British culture was a good thing …

Deciding whether the British Empire was brutal is even more difficult …

People will continue to disagree about the impact of the British Empire because …

CONCLUSION: YOUR VIEWS ON THE BRITISH EMPIRE

Make your views known on a 'Post-it wall'

We've enjoyed producing this book, but it has been a difficult task! The British Empire was so huge; it lasted for such a long time; it included so many different people, ideas and events.

Deciding what to leave out and what to put in our textbook has been a headache. We've tried to include the things that we think were most important to people in the British Empire – both the rulers and the ruled. We've also tried to produce a balanced and fair book. It took lots of discussion amongst ourselves to settle on the topics you see in this book. There were some heated arguments!

We know that this textbook is just our interpretation of the British Empire. Lots of people might want to criticise our interpretation. They might have very different ideas about what to include in a textbook on the British Empire.

How could you leave out some of the great heroes of the British Empire like David Livingstone, General Gordon and Cecil Rhodes?

Why didn't you have a separate enquiry on the American Revolution? It was one of the most important turning points in the history of the British Empire.

You should have included a separate enquiry on Tasmania. What the British did there was terrible!

Your book is nearly all about men. Where are the women?

You haven't included enough information about the way the Empire affected Britain! What about the recent experiences of black and Asian people in Britain?

What about the Opium Wars: smashing into China to force them to buy opium from the British?

We are pleased that people have such strong views about our textbook. At least it shows that:

◆ *history is complicated*

◆ *people care about history*

◆ *history is worth arguing about.*

If it is difficult to write a textbook about the British Empire, then planning a whole museum must be a nightmare! Source 1 shows the new British Empire and Commonwealth Museum in Bristol.

SOURCE 1 The British Empire and Commonwealth Museum, Bristol.

Out of thousands of items which the Museum Director could have put on display, he had to choose only a few hundred. And, having chosen them, what should be said about each one? How should they be arranged?

The Museum Director was obviously aware that the museum was dealing with a controversial topic. Visitors might not agree with what they were shown, or how it was explained. When they get to the end of the exhibition visitors are faced with a 'Post-it wall'. They can write their opinion of the exhibition, or of the Empire, on a Post-it note and stick it on the wall for everyone to read. They can also read what other people have written. You can see from Source 2 that lots of people felt strongly enough to take the trouble to write their own Post-its.

SOURCE 2 The Post-it wall at the British Empire and Commonwealth Museum.

Here are some examples of the things written on the Post-its:

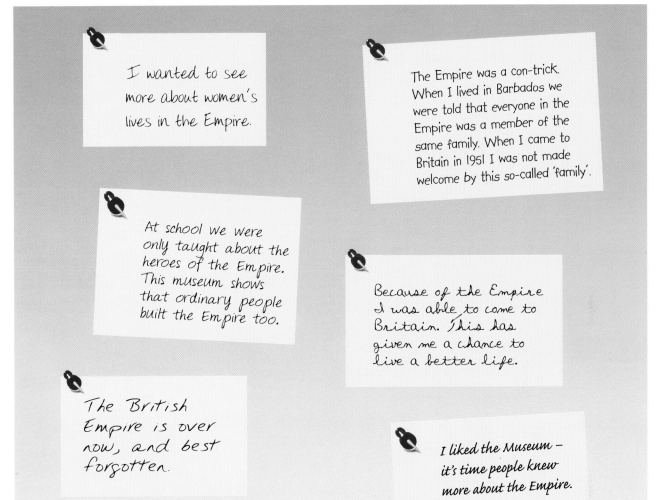

I wanted to see more about women's lives in the Empire.

The Empire was a con-trick. When I lived in Barbados we were told that everyone in the Empire was a member of the same family. When I came to Britain in 1951 I was not made welcome by this so-called 'family'.

At school we were only taught about the heroes of the Empire. This museum shows that ordinary people built the Empire too.

Because of the Empire I was able to come to Britain. This has given me a chance to live a better life.

The British Empire is over now, and best forgotten.

I liked the Museum – it's time people knew more about the Empire.

YOUR POST-ITS

Now it's your turn. Your ideas and views are important too. What would you write on your Post-its to sum up what you really think about the British Empire?

◆ You could write about some of the issues in Chapter 10 of this book. What are *your* views on the impact of empire?
◆ You could write about some of the issues raised in other chapters – look back over the book to remind yourself of the people, places and events you have studied.
◆ You could write about the legacy of the Empire – the experience of black and Asian people in Britain today.

Write some Post-its and put them on your own class Post-it wall.

◆ Glossary

artillery   a section of the army that uses large guns

bilges   the lowest part of the inside of a ship

berth   a fixed bunk on a ship

bush   a wild, uncultivated area of land in Australia

cat o' nine tails   a rope whip with nine knotted lashes used for flogging people

cauterise   to burn the skin in order to stop bleeding

civilisation   a people or nation with a highly organised system of social development

colonists   the people living in a colony

colony   an area of land controlled and inhabited by people from another country

Commonwealth   an association made up of the United Kingdom and states that were previously part of the British Empire

deposed   removed from power

dysentery   a serious disease affecting the intestines

exploited   to be taken advantage of for someone else's benefit

independence   when a country becomes self-governing

Artillery

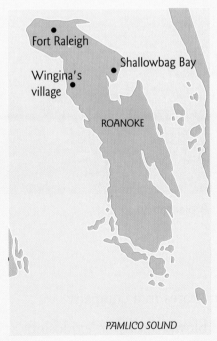

Roanoke: England's first colony in America

minaret a tower connected to a mosque, from where worshippers are called to prayer

musket a light gun supported on the shoulder

patriotic having a strong loyalty to one's country

penal punishment or the means of administering it

pitch a dark sticky substance used for sealing the seams of ships

plantations estates in the colonies where crops were grown on a large scale to be exported around the world. The plantations often used slave labour

provisions stores of food and drink taken on a voyage

scurvy a disease caused by a lack of vitamin C, causing bleeding gums and the opening of previously healed wounds

serfdom a system where some of the people are oppressed and forced to work for others

A minaret

A plantation

shareholders people who own shares in a company

shrapnel fragments of a bomb blown out by an explosion

soothsayers people who can foresee the future and divine the truth

yaws a skin disease causing large red swellings

◆ Index

◆ *Titles in the series*

Pupil's Books (PB) and Teacher's Resource Books (TRB) are available for all titles.

◆ *Acknowledgements*

The Publishers would like to thank the following for permission to reproduce copyright material:

Photographs
Cover Exeter City Museums & Art Gallery; **p.2** Royal Geographical Society, London/ Bridgeman Art Library; **p.3** © The British Museum/Heritage Images; **p.4** *t* Mary Evans Picture Library, *b* Hulton Archive; **p.5** Hulton Archive; **p.6** By courtesy of the National Portrait Gallery, London (NPG 7); **p.13** The Art Archive/British Museum/Harper Collins Publishers; **p.15** The Art Archive/British Museum/Eileen Tweedy; **p.17** © The British Museum/Heritage Images; **p.20** By permission of the British Library; **p.22** © The British Library/Heritage Images; **p.26** Spink & Son Ltd., London/Bridgeman Art Library; **p.28** By courtesy of the National Portrait Gallery, London (NPG 48 – detail); **p.30-31** The Art Archive/General Wolfe Museum Quebec House/Eileen Tweedy; **p.32** National Gallery of Canada, Ottawa; **p.34** National Trust Photographic Library/John Hammond; **p.35** from R.J. Unstead, *Great People of Modern Times*, p.46 (A & C Black Ltd. 1973), photo John Townson/Creation; **p.36** By permission of the British Library; **p.37** R.J. Unstead, *Great People of Modern Times*, p.46 (A & C Black Ltd. 1973), photo John Townson/Creation; **p.38** By courtesy of the National Portrait Gallery, London (NPG 5263 – detail); **p.39** *l* By courtesy of the National Portrait Gallery, London (NPG 48 *f* detail), *r* National Trust Photographic Library/John Hammond; **p.40** Wilberforce House, Hull City Museums and Art Galleries/Bridgeman Art Library; **p.42** Bristol City Museum and Art Gallery/Bridgeman Art Library; **p.44** British Library, London/Bridgeman Art Library; **p.45** *t* British Library, London/ Bridgeman Art Library, *b* British Library, London/Bridgeman Art Library; **p.48** Board of Trustees of the National Museums and Galleries on Merseyside (Walker Art Gallery); **p.49** National Gallery of Canada, Ottawa; **p.50** *t* © Peter M. Fisher/Corbis, *b* Private Collection/ Bridgeman Art Library; **p.51** The Natural History Museum, London; **p.52** Private Collection/Bridgeman Art Library; **p.53** Mary Evans Picture Library; **p.54** *t* Mitchell Library, State Library of New South Wales/Bridgeman Art Library, *b* By permission of the National Library of Australia, Canberra; **p.55** *t* Mitchell Library, State Library of New South Wales, *b* By permission of the National Library of Australia, Canberra; **p.56** Allport Library and Museum of Fine Arts, State Library of Tasmania; **p.58** National Library of Australia, Canberra/Bridgeman Art Library; **p.59** National Library of Australia, Canberra/Bridgeman Art Library; **p.60** By permission of the British Library; **p.62** *t* By courtesy of the National Portrait Gallery, London (NPG 1804 – detail), *b* By permission of the British Library; **p.63** By permission of the British Library;

p.64 *t* Collections/Ken Price, *b* © Bettmann/Corbis; **p.65** By permission of the British Library; **p.66** courtesy of Constable & Robinson Ltd.; **p.68** Stapleton Collection/Bridgeman Art Library; **p.69** By permission of the British Library; **p.70** Punch Library & Archive; **p.72** Hulton Archive; **p.73** Mary Evans Picture Library; **p.74** Exeter City Museums & Art Gallery; **p.77** Hulton Archive; **p.81** Exeter City Museums & Art Gallery; **p.82** © Zen Icknow/Corbis; **p.83** Exeter City Museums & Art Gallery; **p.84** Hulton Archive; **p.85** Somerset Record Office, Taunton; **p.86** Hulton Archive; **p.87** Royal Geographical Society, London/Bridgeman Art Library; **p.88** *t, bl & br* Vin Mag Archive; **p.89** *t & bl* Vin Mag Archive, *br* The Advertising Archive Ltd.; **p.90** *t* Hulton Archive, *b* reproduced by kind permission of The Scout Association; **p.91** *t & b* reproduced by kind permission of The Scout Association; **p.93** *t & b* By permission of the Syndics of Cambridge University Library; **p.94** *t & b* By permission of the Syndics of Cambridge University Library; **p.95** *t & b* By permission of the Syndics of Cambridge University Library; **p.96** *l & r* Hulton Archive; **p.100** © Hulton-Deutsch Collection/Corbis; **p.101** © Hulton-Deutsch Collection/Corbis, *b* © Bettmann/Corbis; **p.103** Hulton Archive; **p.104** Hulton Archive; **p.106** *l* © Ben Judd, *r Empire: The British Imperial Experience from 1765 to the Present* by Denis Judd, cover reproduced by kind permission of Phoenix Press, photo John Townson/Creation; **p.107** *l* © Jerry Bauer, *r* cover reproduced by kind permission of Time Warner Books UK, photo John Townson/Creation; ©; **p.108** reproduced by kind permission of The Leprosy Mission International; **p.109** Private Collection/Bridgeman Art Library; **p.110** *t* Private Collection/Bridgeman Art Library; **p.113** courtesy of the National Library of Jamaica; **p.116** *t & b* The British Empire & Commonwealth Museum; **p.119** British Library, London/Bridgeman Art Library.

(*t* = top, *b* = bottom, *l* = left, *r* = right, *c* = centre)

Written sources
pp.106–107 *BBC History Magazine*

While every effort has been made to contact copyright holders, the Publishers apologise for any omissions, which they will be pleased to rectify at the earliest opportunity.